D1741375

Risk Ownership
Complete Self-Assessment Guide

The guidance in this Self-Assessment is based on Risk Ownership best practices and standards in business process architecture, design and quality management. The guidance is also based on the professional judgment of the individual collaborators listed in the Acknowledgments.

Table of Contents

About The Art of Service

The Art of Service, Business Process Architects since 2000, is dedicated to helping stakeholders achieve excellence.

Defining, designing, creating, and implementing a process to solve a stakeholders challenge or meet an objective is the most valuable role… In EVERY group, company, organization and department.

Unless you're talking a one-time, single-use project, there should be a process. Whether that process is managed and implemented by humans, AI, or a combination of the two, it needs to be designed by someone with a complex enough perspective to ask the right questions.

Someone capable of asking the right questions and step back and say, 'What are we really trying to accomplish here? And is there a different way to look at it?'

With The Art of Service's Standard Requirements Self-Assessments, we empower people who can do just that — whether their title is marketer, entrepreneur, manager, salesperson, consultant, Business Process Manager, executive assistant, IT Manager, CIO etc... —they are the people who rule the future. They are people who watch the process as it happens, and ask the right questions to make the process work better.

Contact us when you need any support with this Self-Assessment and any help with templates, blue-prints and examples of standard documents you might need:

http://theartofservice.com
service@theartofservice.com

Included Resources - how to access

Included with your purchase of the book is the Risk Ownership

Self-Assessment Spreadsheet Dashboard which contains all questions and Self-Assessment areas and auto-generates insights, graphs, and project RACI planning - all with examples to get you started right away.

How? Simply send an email to
access@theartofservice.com
with this books' title in the subject to get the Risk Ownership Self Assessment Tool right away.

You will receive the following contents with New and Updated specific criteria:

- The latest quick edition of the book in PDF

- The latest complete edition of the book in PDF, which criteria correspond to the criteria in...

- The Self-Assessment Excel Dashboard, and...

- Example pre-filled Self-Assessment Excel Dashboard to get familiar with results generation

- In-depth specific Checklists covering the topic

- Project management checklists and templates to assist with implementation

INCLUDES LIFETIME SELF ASSESSMENT UPDATES

Every self assessment comes with Lifetime Updates and Lifetime Free Updated Books. Lifetime Updates is an industry-first feature which allows you to receive verified self assessment updates, ensuring you always have the most accurate information at your fingertips.

Get it now- you will be glad you did - do it now, before you forget.

Send an email to **access@theartofservice.com** with this books' title in the subject to get the Risk Ownership Self Assessment Tool right away.

Purpose of this Self-Assessment

This Self-Assessment has been developed to improve understanding of the requirements and elements of Risk Ownership, based on best practices and standards in business process architecture, design and quality management.

It is designed to allow for a rapid Self-Assessment to determine how closely existing management practices and procedures correspond to the elements of the Self-Assessment.

The criteria of requirements and elements of Risk Ownership have been rephrased in the format of a Self-Assessment questionnaire, with a seven-criterion scoring system, as explained in this document.

In this format, even with limited background knowledge of Risk Ownership, a manager can quickly review existing operations to determine how they measure up to the standards. This in turn can serve as the starting point of a 'gap analysis' to identify management tools or system elements that might usefully be implemented in the organization to help improve overall performance.

How to use the Self-Assessment

On the following pages are a series of questions to identify to what extent your Risk Ownership initiative is complete in comparison to the requirements set in standards.

To facilitate answering the questions, there is a space in front of each question to enter a score on a scale of '1' to '5'.

1 Strongly Disagree

2 Disagree

3 Neutral

4 Agree

5 Strongly Agree

Read the question and rate it with the following in front of mind:

'In my belief, the answer to this question is clearly defined'.

There are two ways in which you can choose to interpret this statement;
1. how aware are you that the answer to the question is clearly defined
2. for more in-depth analysis you can choose to gather evidence and confirm the answer to the question. This obviously will take more time, most Self-Assessment users opt for the first way to interpret the question and dig deeper later on based on the outcome of the overall Self-Assessment.

A score of '1' would mean that the answer is not clear at all, where a '5' would mean the answer is crystal clear and defined. Leave emtpy when the question is not applicable or you don't want to answer it, you can skip it without affecting your score. Write your score in the space provided.

After you have responded to all the appropriate statements in each section, compute your average score for that section, using the formula provided, and round to the nearest tenth. Then transfer to the corresponding spoke in the Risk Ownership Scorecard on the second next page of the Self-Assessment.

Your completed Risk Ownership Scorecard will give you a clear presentation of which Risk Ownership areas need attention.

Risk Ownership
Scorecard Example

Example of how the finalized Scorecard can look like:

Risk Ownership
Scorecard

Your Scores:

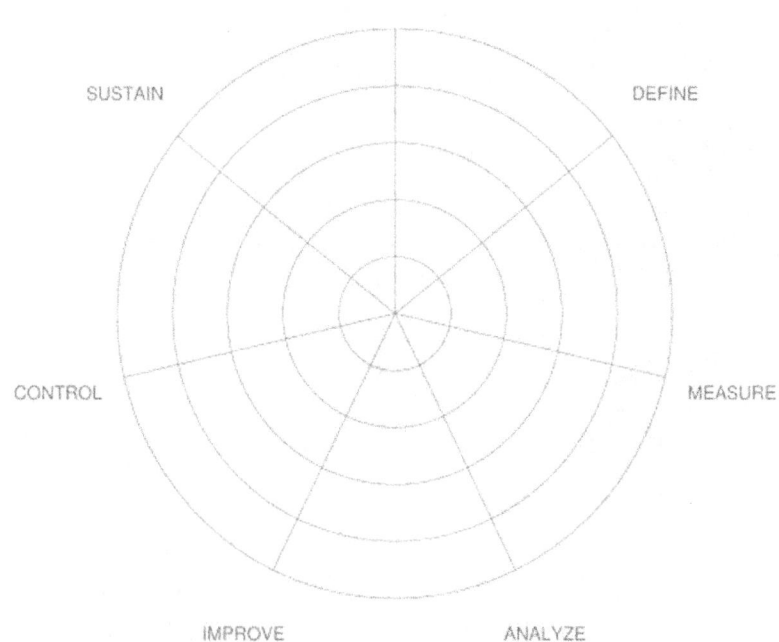

BEGINNING OF THE SELF-ASSESSMENT:

CRITERION #1: RECOGNIZE

INTENT: Be aware of the need for change. Recognize that there is an unfavorable variation, problem or symptom.

In my belief, the answer to this question is clearly defined:

5 Strongly Agree

4 Agree

3 Neutral

2 Disagree

1 Strongly Disagree

1. What extra resources will you need?
<--- Score

2. Are problem definition and motivation clearly presented?
<--- Score

3. What do you need to start doing?
<--- Score

4. What is the smallest subset of the problem you can usefully solve?
<--- Score

5. To what extent would your organization benefit from being recognized as a award recipient?
<--- Score

6. What are the expected benefits of risk ownership to the stakeholder?
<--- Score

7. What problems are you facing and how do you consider risk ownership will circumvent those obstacles?
<--- Score

8. Do you know what you need to know about risk ownership?
<--- Score

9. Does risk ownership create potential expectations in other areas that need to be recognized and considered?
<--- Score

10. Is it needed?
<--- Score

11. Are there recognized risk ownership problems?
<--- Score

12. How do you recognize an risk ownership objection?
<--- Score

13. Does the problem have ethical dimensions?
<--- Score

14. Where is training needed?
<--- Score

15. How are you going to measure success?
<--- Score

16. Are losses recognized in a timely manner?
<--- Score

17. What needs to stay?
<--- Score

18. Are your goals realistic? Do you need to redefine your problem? Perhaps the problem has changed or maybe you have reached your goal and need to set a new one?
<--- Score

19. Who needs to know about risk ownership?
<--- Score

20. Looking at each person individually – does every one have the qualities which are needed to work in this group?
<--- Score

21. Why is this needed?
<--- Score

22. Did you miss any major risk ownership issues?
<--- Score

23. What vendors make products that address the risk ownership needs?

<--- Score

24. What are the minority interests and what amount of minority interests can be recognized?

<--- Score

25. How do you take a forward-looking perspective in identifying risk ownership research related to market response and models?

<--- Score

26. What do employees need in the short term?

<--- Score

27. Which information does the risk ownership business case need to include?

<--- Score

28. When a risk ownership manager recognizes a problem, what options are available?

<--- Score

29. What are the risk ownership resources needed?

<--- Score

30. Who needs budgets?

<--- Score

31. How do you recognize an objection?

<--- Score

32. What else needs to be measured?

<--- Score

33. Are controls defined to recognize and contain problems?
<--- Score

34. How are training requirements identified?
<--- Score

35. What is the recognized need?
<--- Score

36. Are there any specific expectations or concerns about the risk ownership team, risk ownership itself?
<--- Score

37. Which issues are too important to ignore?
<--- Score

38. What training and capacity building actions are needed to implement proposed reforms?
<--- Score

39. For your risk ownership project, identify and describe the business environment, is there more than one layer to the business environment?
<--- Score

40. Do you recognize risk ownership achievements?
<--- Score

41. To what extent does each concerned units management team recognize risk ownership as an effective investment?
<--- Score

42. Do you need different information or graphics?

<--- Score

43. What is the problem and/or vulnerability?
<--- Score

44. What are your needs in relation to risk ownership skills, labor, equipment, and markets?
<--- Score

45. Will it solve real problems?
<--- Score

46. What would happen if risk ownership weren't done?
<--- Score

47. Will risk ownership deliverables need to be tested and, if so, by whom?
<--- Score

48. Where do you need to exercise leadership?
<--- Score

49. Which needs are not included or involved?
<--- Score

50. Who else hopes to benefit from it?
<--- Score

51. Can management personnel recognize the monetary benefit of risk ownership?
<--- Score

52. What risk ownership coordination do you need?
<--- Score

53. What tools and technologies are needed for a custom risk ownership project?

<--- Score

54. What situation(s) led to this risk ownership Self Assessment?

<--- Score

55. What risk ownership events should you attend?

<--- Score

56. Who are your key stakeholders who need to sign off?

<--- Score

57. Do you have/need 24-hour access to key personnel?

<--- Score

58. Do you need to avoid or amend any risk ownership activities?

<--- Score

59. Who needs to know?

<--- Score

60. What risk ownership problem should be solved?

<--- Score

61. What is the extent or complexity of the risk ownership problem?

<--- Score

62. Who should resolve the risk ownership issues?

<--- Score

63. Who needs what information?
<--- Score

64. What information do users need?
<--- Score

65. Will a response program recognize when a crisis occurs and provide some level of response?
<--- Score

66. Whom do you really need or want to serve?
<--- Score

67. Is it clear when you think of the day ahead of you what activities and tasks you need to complete?
<--- Score

68. Think about the people you identified for your risk ownership project and the project responsibilities you would assign to them, what kind of training do you think they would need to perform these responsibilities effectively?
<--- Score

69. How does it fit into your organizational needs and tasks?
<--- Score

70. Will new equipment/products be required to facilitate risk ownership delivery, for example is new software needed?
<--- Score

71. What are the stakeholder objectives to be achieved with risk ownership?
<--- Score

72. Are employees recognized or rewarded for performance that demonstrates the highest levels of integrity?
<--- Score

73. What is the risk ownership problem definition? What do you need to resolve?
<--- Score

74. How can auditing be a preventative security measure?
<--- Score

75. Is the need for organizational change recognized?
<--- Score

76. How much are sponsors, customers, partners, stakeholders involved in risk ownership? In other words, what are the risks, if risk ownership does not deliver successfully?
<--- Score

77. What does risk ownership success mean to the stakeholders?
<--- Score

78. What creative shifts do you need to take?
<--- Score

79. What should be considered when identifying available resources, constraints, and deadlines?
<--- Score

80. Would you recognize a threat from the inside?
<--- Score

81. What are the timeframes required to resolve each of the issues/problems?
<--- Score

82. As a sponsor, customer or management, how important is it to meet goals, objectives?
<--- Score

83. What needs to be done?
<--- Score

84. What is the problem or issue?
<--- Score

85. How are the risk ownership's objectives aligned to the group's overall stakeholder strategy?
<--- Score

86. What prevents you from making the changes you know will make you a more effective risk ownership leader?
<--- Score

87. How do you identify the kinds of information that you will need?
<--- Score

88. Are there any revenue recognition issues?
<--- Score

89. Have you identified your risk ownership key performance indicators?
<--- Score

90. How many trainings, in total, are needed?

<--- Score

91. What activities does the governance board need to consider?
<--- Score

92. Consider your own risk ownership project, what types of organizational problems do you think might be causing or affecting your problem, based on the work done so far?
<--- Score

93. What resources or support might you need?
<--- Score

94. Are you dealing with any of the same issues today as yesterday? What can you do about this?
<--- Score

95. What are the clients issues and concerns?
<--- Score

96. How do you assess your risk ownership workforce capability and capacity needs, including skills, competencies, and staffing levels?
<--- Score

97. Does your organization need more risk ownership education?
<--- Score

98. Are there regulatory / compliance issues?
<--- Score

99. What risk ownership capabilities do you need?
<--- Score

Add up total points for this section:
_ _ _ _ _ = Total points for this section

Divided by: _ _ _ _ _ _ (number of
statements answered) = _ _ _ _ _ _
Average score for this section

Transfer your score to the risk
ownership Index at the beginning of the
Self-Assessment.

CRITERION #2: DEFINE:

INTENT: Formulate the stakeholder problem. Define the problem, needs and objectives.

In my belief, the answer to this question is clearly defined:

5 Strongly Agree

4 Agree

3 Neutral

2 Disagree

1 Strongly Disagree

1. How do you manage unclear risk ownership requirements?
<--- Score

2. What risk ownership requirements should be gathered?
<--- Score

3. Is data collected and displayed to better understand

customer(s) critical needs and requirements.
<--- Score

4. Has a risk ownership requirement not been met?
<--- Score

5. Are different versions of process maps needed to account for the different types of inputs?
<--- Score

6. Is the risk ownership scope manageable?
<--- Score

7. Has anyone else (internal or external to the group) attempted to solve this problem or a similar one before? If so, what knowledge can be leveraged from these previous efforts?
<--- Score

8. Is the team adequately staffed with the desired cross-functionality? If not, what additional resources are available to the team?
<--- Score

9. What risk ownership services do you require?
<--- Score

10. How would you define risk ownership leadership?
<--- Score

11. Who is gathering risk ownership information?
<--- Score

12. What defines best in class?
<--- Score

13. What information should you gather?
<--- Score

14. What are the risk ownership use cases?
<--- Score

15. Is the improvement team aware of the different versions of a process: what they think it is vs. what it actually is vs. what it should be vs. what it could be?
<--- Score

16. How do you build the right business case?
<--- Score

17. How was the 'as is' process map developed, reviewed, verified and validated?
<--- Score

18. Is the current 'as is' process being followed? If not, what are the discrepancies?
<--- Score

19. Has the risk ownership work been fairly and/ or equitably divided and delegated among team members who are qualified and capable to perform the work? Has everyone contributed?
<--- Score

20. What is out-of-scope initially?
<--- Score

21. Is there a completed SIPOC representation, describing the Suppliers, Inputs, Process, Outputs, and Customers?
<--- Score

22. When is the estimated completion date?
<--- Score

23. Why are you doing risk ownership and what is the scope?
<--- Score

24. Are there different segments of customers?
<--- Score

25. What key stakeholder process output measure(s) does risk ownership leverage and how?
<--- Score

26. Are required metrics defined, what are they?
<--- Score

27. Is risk ownership currently on schedule according to the plan?
<--- Score

28. Has your scope been defined?
<--- Score

29. Is the work to date meeting requirements?
<--- Score

30. How do you catch risk ownership definition inconsistencies?
<--- Score

31. What is out of scope?
<--- Score

32. Is there a completed, verified, and validated high-level 'as is' (not 'should be' or 'could be') stakeholder

process map?
<--- Score

33. How does the risk ownership manager ensure against scope creep?
<--- Score

34. If substitutes have been appointed, have they been briefed on the risk ownership goals and received regular communications as to the progress to date?
<--- Score

35. Will team members perform risk ownership work when assigned and in a timely fashion?
<--- Score

36. What are the requirements for audit information?
<--- Score

37. How are consistent risk ownership definitions important?
<--- Score

38. Where can you gather more information?
<--- Score

39. What are the rough order estimates on cost savings/opportunities that risk ownership brings?
<--- Score

40. How would you define the culture at your organization, how susceptible is it to risk ownership changes?
<--- Score

41. Does the team have regular meetings?
<--- Score

42. Are all requirements met?
<--- Score

43. How do you gather risk ownership requirements?
<--- Score

44. How did the risk ownership manager receive input to the development of a risk ownership improvement plan and the estimated completion dates/times of each activity?
<--- Score

45. Is there a risk ownership management charter, including stakeholder case, problem and goal statements, scope, milestones, roles and responsibilities, communication plan?
<--- Score

46. What sort of initial information to gather?
<--- Score

47. How will variation in the actual durations of each activity be dealt with to ensure that the expected risk ownership results are met?
<--- Score

48. What sources do you use to gather information for a risk ownership study?
<--- Score

49. How and when will the baselines be defined?
<--- Score

50. Have specific policy objectives been defined?
<--- Score

51. Do you have a risk ownership success story or case study ready to tell and share?
<--- Score

52. When are meeting minutes sent out? Who is on the distribution list?
<--- Score

53. How do you manage scope?
<--- Score

54. Is there a critical path to deliver risk ownership results?
<--- Score

55. How will the risk ownership team and the group measure complete success of risk ownership?
<--- Score

56. Do the problem and goal statements meet the SMART criteria (specific, measurable, attainable, relevant, and time-bound)?
<--- Score

57. What are the tasks and definitions?
<--- Score

58. Are customer(s) identified and segmented according to their different needs and requirements?
<--- Score

59. Are the risk ownership requirements complete?
<--- Score

60. What is the scope of risk ownership?
<--- Score

61. What are the risk ownership tasks and definitions?
<--- Score

62. What was the context?
<--- Score

63. Who is gathering information?
<--- Score

64. Who approved the risk ownership scope?
<--- Score

65. What are (control) requirements for risk ownership Information?
<--- Score

66. What is the scope?
<--- Score

67. What specifically is the problem? Where does it occur? When does it occur? What is its extent?
<--- Score

68. What would be the goal or target for a risk ownership's improvement team?
<--- Score

69. Will team members regularly document their risk ownership work?
<--- Score

70. What scope do you want your strategy to cover?

<--- Score

71. Has the improvement team collected the 'voice of the customer' (obtained feedback – qualitative and quantitative)?
<--- Score

72. Has a project plan, Gantt chart, or similar been developed/completed?
<--- Score

73. Do you all define risk ownership in the same way?
<--- Score

74. What is the context?
<--- Score

75. What is the scope of the risk ownership work?
<--- Score

76. What is a worst-case scenario for losses?
<--- Score

77. Is there any additional risk ownership definition of success?
<--- Score

78. What happens if risk ownership's scope changes?
<--- Score

79. What scope to assess?
<--- Score

80. What are the record-keeping requirements of risk ownership activities?
<--- Score

81. How have you defined all risk ownership requirements first?

<--- Score

82. When is/was the risk ownership start date?

<--- Score

83. How do you think the partners involved in risk ownership would have defined success?

<--- Score

84. What information do you gather?

<--- Score

85. What are the Roles and Responsibilities for each team member and its leadership? Where is this documented?

<--- Score

86. Are approval levels defined for contracts and supplements to contracts?

<--- Score

87. What is the definition of risk ownership excellence?

<--- Score

88. What is the worst case scenario?

<--- Score

89. Are task requirements clearly defined?

<--- Score

90. Scope of sensitive information?

<--- Score

91. Has a high-level 'as is' process map been completed, verified and validated?
<--- Score

92. Is there regularly 100% attendance at the team meetings? If not, have appointed substitutes attended to preserve cross-functionality and full representation?
<--- Score

93. Have the customer needs been translated into specific, measurable requirements? How?
<--- Score

94. Does the scope remain the same?
<--- Score

95. Has the direction changed at all during the course of risk ownership? If so, when did it change and why?
<--- Score

96. Will a risk ownership production readiness review be required?
<--- Score

97. What is in scope?
<--- Score

98. Has/have the customer(s) been identified?
<--- Score

99. The political context: who holds power?
<--- Score

100. In what way can you redefine the criteria of

choice clients have in your category in your favor?
<--- Score

101. How do you gather requirements?
<--- Score

102. What constraints exist that might impact the team?
<--- Score

103. Are accountability and ownership for risk ownership clearly defined?
<--- Score

104. What intelligence can you gather?
<--- Score

105. Are resources adequate for the scope?
<--- Score

106. What customer feedback methods were used to solicit their input?
<--- Score

107. Who defines (or who defined) the rules and roles?
<--- Score

108. What are the dynamics of the communication plan?
<--- Score

109. What is the scope of the risk ownership effort?
<--- Score

110. Are audit criteria, scope, frequency and

methods defined?
<--- Score

111. Is risk ownership linked to key stakeholder goals and objectives?
<--- Score

112. What gets examined?
<--- Score

113. How do you keep key subject matter experts in the loop?
<--- Score

114. What are the boundaries of the scope? What is in bounds and what is not? What is the start point? What is the stop point?
<--- Score

115. Has a team charter been developed and communicated?
<--- Score

116. What baselines are required to be defined and managed?
<--- Score

117. What is in the scope and what is not in scope?
<--- Score

118. Are roles and responsibilities formally defined?
<--- Score

119. Is there a clear risk ownership case definition?
<--- Score

120. Are there any constraints known that bear on the ability to perform risk ownership work? How is the team addressing them?
<--- Score

121. Is the scope of risk ownership defined?
<--- Score

122. What system do you use for gathering risk ownership information?
<--- Score

123. How often are the team meetings?
<--- Score

124. What are the compelling stakeholder reasons for embarking on risk ownership?
<--- Score

125. What are the core elements of the risk ownership business case?
<--- Score

126. Who are the risk ownership improvement team members, including Management Leads and Coaches?
<--- Score

127. How do you manage changes in risk ownership requirements?
<--- Score

128. What critical content must be communicated – who, what, when, where, and how?
<--- Score

129. Is the risk ownership scope complete and appropriately sized?
<--- Score

130. Is it clearly defined in and to your organization what you do?
<--- Score

131. Has everyone on the team, including the team leaders, been properly trained?
<--- Score

132. How is the team tracking and documenting its work?
<--- Score

133. How can the value of risk ownership be defined?
<--- Score

134. Do you have organizational privacy requirements?
<--- Score

135. Have all basic functions of risk ownership been defined?
<--- Score

136. How do you gather the stories?
<--- Score

137. Is the team equipped with available and reliable resources?
<--- Score

Add up total points for this section:
_ _ _ _ _ = Total points for this section

Divided by: _____ (number of
statements answered) = _____
Average score for this section

Transfer your score to the risk
ownership Index at the beginning of the
Self-Assessment.

CRITERION #3: MEASURE:

INTENT: Gather the correct data.
Measure the current performance and
evolution of the situation.

In my belief, the answer to this
question is clearly defined:

5 Strongly Agree

4 Agree

3 Neutral

2 Disagree

1 Strongly Disagree

1. What does your operating model cost?
<--- Score

2. Who is involved in verifying compliance?
<--- Score

3. What are you verifying?
<--- Score

4. How do you verify and develop ideas and innovations?
<--- Score

5. How do you measure success?
<--- Score

6. Have you included everything in your risk ownership cost models?
<--- Score

7. Are supply costs steady or fluctuating?
<--- Score

8. What harm might be caused?
<--- Score

9. How will you measure your risk ownership effectiveness?
<--- Score

10. What are the strategic priorities for this year?
<--- Score

11. What causes extra work or rework?
<--- Score

12. What do you measure and why?
<--- Score

13. How frequently do you track risk ownership measures?
<--- Score

14. What evidence is there and what is measured?
<--- Score

15. What are the risk ownership key cost drivers?
<--- Score

16. Has a cost center been established?
<--- Score

17. Have design-to-cost goals been established?
<--- Score

18. How to cause the change?
<--- Score

19. What are the costs?
<--- Score

20. What are the uncertainties surrounding estimates of impact?
<--- Score

21. How much does it cost?
<--- Score

22. What is the cause of any risk ownership gaps?
<--- Score

23. How is performance measured?
<--- Score

24. How do you quantify and qualify impacts?
<--- Score

25. How can you measure the performance?
<--- Score

26. Are the measurements objective?

<--- Score

27. What drives O&M cost?
<--- Score

28. Will risk ownership have an impact on current business continuity, disaster recovery processes and/or infrastructure?
<--- Score

29. What causes investor action?
<--- Score

30. Are indirect costs charged to the risk ownership program?
<--- Score

31. What are your primary costs, revenues, assets?
<--- Score

32. What potential environmental factors impact the risk ownership effort?
<--- Score

33. How is the value delivered by risk ownership being measured?
<--- Score

34. What is the cost of rework?
<--- Score

35. How do you measure variability?
<--- Score

36. Are you aware of what could cause a problem?
<--- Score

37. What is measured? Why?
<--- Score

38. What can be used to verify compliance?
<--- Score

39. Are missed risk ownership opportunities costing your organization money?
<--- Score

40. What is the root cause(s) of the problem?
<--- Score

41. How do your measurements capture actionable risk ownership information for use in exceeding your customers expectations and securing your customers engagement?
<--- Score

42. What are the costs of reform?
<--- Score

43. How do you focus on what is right -not who is right?
<--- Score

44. How will measures be used to manage and adapt?
<--- Score

45. What are the costs of delaying risk ownership action?
<--- Score

46. What are your customers expectations and measures?

<--- Score

47. What do people want to verify?
<--- Score

48. What could cause delays in the schedule?
<--- Score

49. Did you tackle the cause or the symptom?
<--- Score

50. How do you measure lifecycle phases?
<--- Score

51. Does management have the right priorities among projects?
<--- Score

52. What causes mismanagement?
<--- Score

53. What is your risk ownership quality cost segregation study?
<--- Score

54. How will your organization measure success?
<--- Score

55. Where is it measured?
<--- Score

56. Where can you go to verify the info?
<--- Score

57. What details are required of the risk ownership cost structure?

<--- Score

58. What are hidden risk ownership quality costs?
<--- Score

59. What is the total fixed cost?
<--- Score

60. What does losing customers cost your organization?
<--- Score

61. Is the solution cost-effective?
<--- Score

62. How do you verify performance?
<--- Score

63. How do you verify and validate the risk ownership data?
<--- Score

64. Where is the cost?
<--- Score

65. How do you prevent mis-estimating cost?
<--- Score

66. Who should receive measurement reports?
<--- Score

67. Are risk ownership vulnerabilities categorized and prioritized?
<--- Score

68. Who pays the cost?

<--- Score

69. Do you have a flow diagram of what happens?
<--- Score

70. What measurements are being captured?
<--- Score

71. **What are the risk ownership investment costs?**
<--- Score

72. How can you measure risk ownership in a systematic way?
<--- Score

73. What is an unallowable cost?
<--- Score

74. **How do you aggregate measures across priorities?**
<--- Score

75. What are the operational costs after risk ownership deployment?
<--- Score

76. What does a Test Case verify?
<--- Score

77. What are your operating costs?
<--- Score

78. How do you stay flexible and focused to recognize larger risk ownership results?
<--- Score

79. What happens if cost savings do not materialize?

<--- Score

80. What methods are feasible and acceptable to estimate the impact of reforms?

<--- Score

81. Among the risk ownership product and service cost to be estimated, which is considered hardest to estimate?

<--- Score

82. What relevant entities could be measured?

<--- Score

83. How will you measure success?

<--- Score

84. Do you have an issue in getting priority?

<--- Score

85. How sensitive must the risk ownership strategy be to cost?

<--- Score

86. What tests verify requirements?

<--- Score

87. What are the costs and benefits?

<--- Score

88. Is it possible to estimate the impact of unanticipated complexity such as wrong or failed assumptions, feedback, etcetera on proposed reforms?

<--- Score

89. What disadvantage does this cause for the user?
<--- Score

90. What does verifying compliance entail?
<--- Score

91. How are you verifying it?
<--- Score

92. Does a risk ownership quantification method exist?
<--- Score

93. Are there competing risk ownership priorities?
<--- Score

94. How do you verify your resources?
<--- Score

95. What are the types and number of measures to use?
<--- Score

96. How will success or failure be measured?
<--- Score

97. Are the risk ownership benefits worth its costs?
<--- Score

98. How can you reduce costs?
<--- Score

99. How can you reduce the costs of obtaining inputs?
<--- Score

100. Was a business case (cost/benefit) developed?
<--- Score

101. Are there measurements based on task performance?
<--- Score

102. Are you taking your company in the direction of better and revenue or cheaper and cost?
<--- Score

103. Is the cost worth the risk ownership effort ?
<--- Score

104. How long to keep data and how to manage retention costs?
<--- Score

105. Are actual costs in line with budgeted costs?
<--- Score

106. When should you bother with diagrams?
<--- Score

107. Are there any easy-to-implement alternatives to risk ownership? Sometimes other solutions are available that do not require the cost implications of a full-blown project?
<--- Score

108. Do you verify that corrective actions were taken?
<--- Score

109. What could cause you to change course?
<--- Score

110. Do you aggressively reward and promote the people who have the biggest impact on creating excellent risk ownership services/products?
<--- Score

111. What are your key risk ownership organizational performance measures, including key short and longer-term financial measures?
<--- Score

112. How do you verify the authenticity of the data and information used?
<--- Score

113. How are measurements made?
<--- Score

114. What is the total cost related to deploying risk ownership, including any consulting or professional services?
<--- Score

115. How will effects be measured?
<--- Score

116. Do you have any cost risk ownership limitation requirements?
<--- Score

117. How are costs allocated?
<--- Score

118. How is progress measured?
<--- Score

119. Why do you expend time and effort to implement measurement, for whom?
<--- Score

120. How can you manage cost down?
<--- Score

121. The approach of traditional risk ownership works for detail complexity but is focused on a systematic approach rather than an understanding of the nature of systems themselves, what approach will permit your organization to deal with the kind of unpredictable emergent behaviors that dynamic complexity can introduce?
<--- Score

122. Do the benefits outweigh the costs?
<--- Score

123. Are the units of measure consistent?
<--- Score

124. Why do the measurements/indicators matter?
<--- Score

125. Why a risk ownership focus?
<--- Score

126. Is there an opportunity to verify requirements?
<--- Score

127. How will costs be allocated?
<--- Score

128. How do you verify the risk ownership requirements quality?

<--- Score

129. At what cost?
<--- Score

130. What would it cost to replace your technology?
<--- Score

131. How do you verify if risk ownership is built right?
<--- Score

132. What are allowable costs?
<--- Score

133. What are the estimated costs of proposed changes?
<--- Score

134. What causes innovation to fail or succeed in your organization?
<--- Score

135. Have you made assumptions about the shape of the future, particularly its impact on your customers and competitors?
<--- Score

136. How can a risk ownership test verify your ideas or assumptions?
<--- Score

Add up total points for this section:
_ _ _ _ _ = Total points for this section

Divided by: _ _ _ _ _ _ (number of
statements answered) = _ _ _ _ _ _

Average score for this section

Transfer your score to the risk
ownership Index at the beginning of the
Self-Assessment.

CRITERION #4: ANALYZE:

INTENT: Analyze causes, assumptions and hypotheses.

In my belief, the answer to this question is clearly defined:

5 Strongly Agree

4 Agree

3 Neutral

2 Disagree

1 Strongly Disagree

1. How do you promote understanding that opportunity for improvement is not criticism of the status quo, or the people who created the status quo?
<--- Score

2. How is risk ownership data gathered?
<--- Score

3. Are your outputs consistent?

<--- Score

4. What will drive risk ownership change?
<--- Score

5. What is the complexity of the output produced?
<--- Score

6. What are evaluation criteria for the output?
<--- Score

7. What are the risk ownership design outputs?
<--- Score

8. How can risk management be tied procedurally to process elements?
<--- Score

9. Who is involved in the management review process?
<--- Score

10. What are the risk ownership business drivers?
<--- Score

11. Who will facilitate the team and process?
<--- Score

12. Do you understand your management processes today?
<--- Score

13. Have any additional benefits been identified that will result from closing all or most of the gaps?
<--- Score

14. What are your outputs?
<--- Score

15. What is your organizations system for selecting qualified vendors?
<--- Score

16. What qualifies as competition?
<--- Score

17. What risk ownership metrics are outputs of the process?
<--- Score

18. What resources go in to get the desired output?
<--- Score

19. How was the detailed process map generated, verified, and validated?
<--- Score

20. Who qualifies to gain access to data?
<--- Score

21. How is the risk ownership Value Stream Mapping managed?
<--- Score

22. Do several people in different organizational units assist with the risk ownership process?
<--- Score

23. Can you add value to the current risk ownership decision-making process (largely qualitative) by incorporating uncertainty modeling (more quantitative)?

<--- Score

24. Think about some of the processes you undertake within your organization, which do you own?
<--- Score

25. What qualifications do risk ownership leaders need?
<--- Score

26. Is data and process analysis, root cause analysis and quantifying the gap/opportunity in place?
<--- Score

27. Where is the data coming from to measure compliance?
<--- Score

28. Were there any improvement opportunities identified from the process analysis?
<--- Score

29. Were Pareto charts (or similar) used to portray the 'heavy hitters' (or key sources of variation)?
<--- Score

30. Has an output goal been set?
<--- Score

31. How do you measure the operational performance of your key work systems and processes, including productivity, cycle time, and other appropriate measures of process effectiveness, efficiency, and innovation?
<--- Score

32. Who will gather what data?
<--- Score

33. What are the disruptive risk ownership technologies that enable your organization to radically change your business processes?
<--- Score

34. How often will data be collected for measures?
<--- Score

35. Which risk ownership data should be retained?
<--- Score

36. Is the final output clearly identified?
<--- Score

37. What other jobs or tasks affect the performance of the steps in the risk ownership process?
<--- Score

38. What successful thing are you doing today that may be blinding you to new growth opportunities?
<--- Score

39. Is the risk ownership process severely broken such that a re-design is necessary?
<--- Score

40. What conclusions were drawn from the team's data collection and analysis? How did the team reach these conclusions?
<--- Score

41. What were the financial benefits resulting from any 'ground fruit or low-hanging fruit' (quick fixes)?

<--- Score

42. Who is involved with workflow mapping?
<--- Score

43. A compounding model resolution with available relevant data can often provide insight towards a solution methodology; which risk ownership models, tools and techniques are necessary?
<--- Score

44. Where is risk ownership data gathered?
<--- Score

45. What is the oversight process?
<--- Score

46. Was a cause-and-effect diagram used to explore the different types of causes (or sources of variation)?
<--- Score

47. What methods do you use to gather risk ownership data?
<--- Score

48. Are risk ownership changes recognized early enough to be approved through the regular process?
<--- Score

49. How has the risk ownership data been gathered?
<--- Score

50. What is the risk ownership Driver?
<--- Score

51. What qualifications are necessary?
<--- Score

52. Are all staff in core risk ownership subjects Highly Qualified?
<--- Score

53. What are your current levels and trends in key risk ownership measures or indicators of product and process performance that are important to and directly serve your customers?
<--- Score

54. An organizationally feasible system request is one that considers the mission, goals and objectives of the organization, key questions are: is the risk ownership solution request practical and will it solve a problem or take advantage of an opportunity to achieve company goals?
<--- Score

55. Do quality systems drive continuous improvement?
<--- Score

56. What process should you select for improvement?
<--- Score

57. What are your risk ownership processes?
<--- Score

58. Think about the functions involved in your risk ownership project, what processes flow from these functions?

<--- Score

59. What risk ownership data will be collected?
<--- Score

60. Is pre-qualification of suppliers carried out?
<--- Score

61. What tools were used to narrow the list of possible causes?
<--- Score

62. What data is gathered?
<--- Score

63. How is the data gathered?
<--- Score

64. What other organizational variables, such as reward systems or communication systems, affect the performance of this risk ownership process?
<--- Score

65. Are all team members qualified for all tasks?
<--- Score

66. When should a process be art not science?
<--- Score

67. Do you, as a leader, bounce back quickly from setbacks?
<--- Score

68. Is there any way to speed up the process?
<--- Score

69. What are the revised rough estimates of the financial savings/opportunity for risk ownership improvements?
<--- Score

70. Who gets your output?
<--- Score

71. Do your employees have the opportunity to do what they do best everyday?
<--- Score

72. What do you need to qualify?
<--- Score

73. Did any value-added analysis or 'lean thinking' take place to identify some of the gaps shown on the 'as is' process map?
<--- Score

74. Has data output been validated?
<--- Score

75. What are the processes for audit reporting and management?
<--- Score

76. What are the necessary qualifications?
<--- Score

77. What, related to, risk ownership processes does your organization outsource?
<--- Score

78. What types of data do your risk ownership indicators require?

<--- Score

79. How do you ensure that the risk ownership opportunity is realistic?
<--- Score

80. What does the data say about the performance of the stakeholder process?
<--- Score

81. What is the cost of poor quality as supported by the team's analysis?
<--- Score

82. Are you missing risk ownership opportunities?
<--- Score

83. How will the data be checked for quality?
<--- Score

84. How will the risk ownership data be captured?
<--- Score

85. What kind of crime could a potential new hire have committed that would not only not disqualify him/her from being hired by your organization, but would actually indicate that he/she might be a particularly good fit?
<--- Score

86. What systems/processes must you excel at?
<--- Score

87. What is the output?
<--- Score

88. What risk ownership data do you gather or use now?
<--- Score

89. Were any designed experiments used to generate additional insight into the data analysis?
<--- Score

90. Who owns what data?
<--- Score

91. How is the way you as the leader think and process information affecting your organizational culture?
<--- Score

92. Is the gap/opportunity displayed and communicated in financial terms?
<--- Score

93. What quality tools were used to get through the analyze phase?
<--- Score

94. What information qualified as important?
<--- Score

95. Do your leaders quickly bounce back from setbacks?
<--- Score

96. What training and qualifications will you need?
<--- Score

97. What output to create?
<--- Score

98. What are your current levels and trends in key measures or indicators of risk ownership product and process performance that are important to and directly serve your customers? How do these results compare with the performance of your competitors and other organizations with similar offerings?
<--- Score

99. What are the personnel training and qualifications required?
<--- Score

100. How do you implement and manage your work processes to ensure that they meet design requirements?
<--- Score

101. Did any additional data need to be collected?
<--- Score

102. How much data can be collected in the given timeframe?
<--- Score

103. How are outputs preserved and protected?
<--- Score

104. What risk ownership data should be managed?
<--- Score

105. Should you invest in industry-recognized qualifications?
<--- Score

106. Do you have the authority to produce the

output?
<--- Score

107. How do you use risk ownership data and information to support organizational decision making and innovation?
<--- Score

108. How do you identify specific risk ownership investment opportunities and emerging trends?
<--- Score

109. How is data used for program management and improvement?
<--- Score

110. What are the best opportunities for value improvement?
<--- Score

111. What are your best practices for minimizing risk ownership project risk, while demonstrating incremental value and quick wins throughout the risk ownership project lifecycle?
<--- Score

112. How do you define collaboration and team output?
<--- Score

113. Have you defined which data is gathered how?
<--- Score

114. How do your work systems and key work processes relate to and capitalize on your core competencies?

<--- Score

115. What did the team gain from developing a sub-process map?
<--- Score

116. Is the suppliers process defined and controlled?
<--- Score

117. Identify an operational issue in your organization, for example, could a particular task be done more quickly or more efficiently by risk ownership?
<--- Score

118. What process improvements will be needed?
<--- Score

119. How difficult is it to qualify what risk ownership ROI is?
<--- Score

120. What controls do you have in place to protect data?
<--- Score

121. Was a detailed process map created to amplify critical steps of the 'as is' stakeholder process?
<--- Score

122. What internal processes need improvement?
<--- Score

123. Is the performance gap determined?
<--- Score

124. What data do you need to collect?

<--- Score

125. How will the change process be managed?
<--- Score

126. What are your key performance measures or indicators and in-process measures for the control and improvement of your risk ownership processes?
<--- Score

127. What is your organizations process which leads to recognition of value generation?
<--- Score

128. How many input/output points does it require?
<--- Score

129. What were the crucial 'moments of truth' on the process map?
<--- Score

130. How does the organization define, manage, and improve its risk ownership processes?
<--- Score

131. How do mission and objectives affect the risk ownership processes of your organization?
<--- Score

132. Is there a strict change management process?
<--- Score

133. What qualifications are needed?
<--- Score

134. Have the problem and goal statements been

updated to reflect the additional knowledge gained from the analyze phase?

<--- Score

135. Do staff qualifications match your project?

<--- Score

136. Are gaps between current performance and the goal performance identified?

<--- Score

137. What tools were used to generate the list of possible causes?

<--- Score

Add up total points for this section:
_ _ _ _ _ = Total points for this section

Divided by: _ _ _ _ _ _ (number of statements answered) = _ _ _ _ _ _
Average score for this section

Transfer your score to the risk ownership Index at the beginning of the Self-Assessment.

CRITERION #5: IMPROVE:

INTENT: Develop a practical solution. Innovate, establish and test the solution and to measure the results.

In my belief, the answer to this question is clearly defined:

5 Strongly Agree

4 Agree

3 Neutral

2 Disagree

1 Strongly Disagree

1. Are the key business and technology risks being managed?
<--- Score

2. What is the risk?
<--- Score

3. Which risk ownership solution is appropriate?
<--- Score

4. How are policy decisions made and where?
<--- Score

5. Is risk periodically assessed?
<--- Score

6. What are the implications of the one critical risk ownership decision 10 minutes, 10 months, and 10 years from now?
<--- Score

7. Is the solution technically practical?
<--- Score

8. How does your organization evaluate strategic risk ownership success?
<--- Score

9. Risk Identification: What are the possible risk events your organization faces in relation to risk ownership?
<--- Score

10. What do you want to improve?
<--- Score

11. Is pilot data collected and analyzed?
<--- Score

12. What to do with the results or outcomes of measurements?
<--- Score

13. Does a good decision guarantee a good outcome?
<--- Score

14. What tools were used to tap into the creativity and encourage 'outside the box' thinking?
<--- Score

15. Is the risk ownership solution sustainable?
<--- Score

16. Do those selected for the risk ownership team have a good general understanding of what risk ownership is all about?
<--- Score

17. How do you improve risk ownership service perception, and satisfaction?
<--- Score

18. Who should make the risk ownership decisions?
<--- Score

19. How do you go about comparing risk ownership approaches/solutions?
<--- Score

20. Is there a high likelihood that any recommendations will achieve their intended results?
<--- Score

21. How do you manage risk ownership risk?
<--- Score

22. Can the solution be designed and implemented within an acceptable time period?
<--- Score

23. Is a solution implementation plan established,

including schedule/work breakdown structure, resources, risk management plan, cost/budget, and control plan?
<--- Score

24. How are risk ownership risks managed?
<--- Score

25. Why improve in the first place?
<--- Score

26. To what extent does management recognize risk ownership as a tool to increase the results?
<--- Score

27. Was a pilot designed for the proposed solution(s)?
<--- Score

28. Do you need to do a usability evaluation?
<--- Score

29. Are decisions made in a timely manner?
<--- Score

30. Can you identify any significant risks or exposures to risk ownership third- parties (vendors, service providers, alliance partners etc) that concern you?
<--- Score

31. How do you link measurement and risk?
<--- Score

32. Are events managed to resolution?
<--- Score

33. What is the team's contingency plan for potential

problems occurring in implementation?
<--- Score

34. Are you assessing risk ownership and risk?
<--- Score

35. What communications are necessary to support the implementation of the solution?
<--- Score

36. Is the risk ownership risk managed?
<--- Score

37. Do you have the optimal project management team structure?
<--- Score

38. What current systems have to be understood and/or changed?
<--- Score

39. Is the measure of success for risk ownership understandable to a variety of people?
<--- Score

40. How will you know when its improved?
<--- Score

41. Will the controls trigger any other risks?
<--- Score

42. Is the scope clearly documented?
<--- Score

43. What area needs the greatest improvement?
<--- Score

44. Are the risks fully understood, reasonable and manageable?
<--- Score

45. Who will be responsible for documenting the risk ownership requirements in detail?
<--- Score

46. What are the risk ownership security risks?
<--- Score

47. How do you measure improved risk ownership service perception, and satisfaction?
<--- Score

48. Does the goal represent a desired result that can be measured?
<--- Score

49. Who are the risk ownership decision makers?
<--- Score

50. How do you decide how much to remunerate an employee?
<--- Score

51. Is there any other risk ownership solution?
<--- Score

52. What does the 'should be' process map/design look like?
<--- Score

53. Is there a cost/benefit analysis of optimal solution(s)?

<--- Score

54. What resources are required for the improvement efforts?

<--- Score

55. Who will be using the results of the measurement activities?

<--- Score

56. How can you improve risk ownership?

<--- Score

57. At what point will vulnerability assessments be performed once risk ownership is put into production (e.g., ongoing Risk Management after implementation)?

<--- Score

58. What error proofing will be done to address some of the discrepancies observed in the 'as is' process?

<--- Score

59. In the past few months, what is the smallest change you have made that has had the biggest positive result? What was it about that small change that produced the large return?

<--- Score

60. Risk events: what are the things that could go wrong?

<--- Score

61. Risk factors: what are the characteristics of risk ownership that make it risky?

<--- Score

62. Is the optimal solution selected based on testing and analysis?
<--- Score

63. Which of the recognised risks out of all risks can be most likely transferred?
<--- Score

64. How risky is your organization?
<--- Score

65. Was a risk ownership charter developed?
<--- Score

66. What practices helps your organization to develop its capacity to recognize patterns?
<--- Score

67. How will you know that you have improved?
<--- Score

68. What are the expected risk ownership results?
<--- Score

69. What alternative responses are available to manage risk?
<--- Score

70. How do you manage and improve your risk ownership work systems to deliver customer value and achieve organizational success and sustainability?
<--- Score

71. Are risk triggers captured?
<--- Score

72. Can you integrate quality management and risk management?
<--- Score

73. What are the concrete risk ownership results?
<--- Score

74. Do vendor agreements bring new compliance risk ?
<--- Score

75. For decision problems, how do you develop a decision statement?
<--- Score

76. What strategies for risk ownership improvement are successful?
<--- Score

77. How can the phases of risk ownership development be identified?
<--- Score

78. How do you measure risk?
<--- Score

79. Who do you report risk ownership results to?
<--- Score

80. What tools were used to evaluate the potential solutions?
<--- Score

81. What assumptions are made about the solution and approach?

<--- Score

82. Who are the people involved in developing and implementing risk ownership?
<--- Score

83. What went well, what should change, what can improve?
<--- Score

84. How can skill-level changes improve risk ownership?
<--- Score

85. What tools do you use once you have decided on a risk ownership strategy and more importantly how do you choose?
<--- Score

86. What risks do you need to manage?
<--- Score

87. Would you develop a risk ownership Communication Strategy?
<--- Score

88. Have you identified breakpoints and/or risk tolerances that will trigger broad consideration of a potential need for intervention or modification of strategy?
<--- Score

89. Do you cover the five essential competencies: Communication, Collaboration,Innovation, Adaptability, and Leadership that improve an organizations ability to leverage the new risk

ownership in a volatile global economy?
<--- Score

90. What improvements have been achieved?
<--- Score

91. How will you know that a change is an improvement?
<--- Score

92. How do you measure progress and evaluate training effectiveness?
<--- Score

93. For estimation problems, how do you develop an estimation statement?
<--- Score

94. How do you keep improving risk ownership?
<--- Score

95. Who will be responsible for making the decisions to include or exclude requested changes once risk ownership is underway?
<--- Score

96. Is the implementation plan designed?
<--- Score

97. Do you combine technical expertise with business knowledge and risk ownership Key topics include lifecycles, development approaches, requirements and how to make a business case?
<--- Score

98. What lessons, if any, from a pilot were

incorporated into the design of the full-scale solution?
<--- Score

99. What needs improvement? Why?
<--- Score

100. What actually has to improve and by how much?
<--- Score

101. What criteria will you use to assess your risk ownership risks?
<--- Score

102. What were the criteria for evaluating a risk ownership pilot?
<--- Score

103. What is risk ownership's impact on utilizing the best solution(s)?
<--- Score

104. Who manages risk ownership risk?
<--- Score

105. How will you measure the results?
<--- Score

106. Have you achieved risk ownership improvements?
<--- Score

107. Where do you need risk ownership improvement?
<--- Score

108. What is the risk ownership's sustainability risk?

<--- Score

109. What are your current levels and trends in key measures or indicators of workforce and leader development?
<--- Score

110. How is knowledge sharing about risk management improved?
<--- Score

111. If you could go back in time five years, what decision would you make differently? What is your best guess as to what decision you're making today you might regret five years from now?
<--- Score

112. Are procedures documented for managing risk ownership risks?
<--- Score

113. What is the magnitude of the improvements?
<--- Score

114. Is a contingency plan established?
<--- Score

115. How do you improve your likelihood of success ?
<--- Score

116. What is the implementation plan?
<--- Score

117. Explorations of the frontiers of risk ownership will help you build influence, improve risk ownership,

optimize decision making, and sustain change, what is your approach?

<--- Score

118. How can you better manage risk?

<--- Score

119. How significant is the improvement in the eyes of the end user?

<--- Score

120. How do you improve productivity?

<--- Score

121. What tools were most useful during the improve phase?

<--- Score

122. risk ownership risk decisions: whose call Is It?

<--- Score

123. What are the affordable risk ownership risks?

<--- Score

124. Were any criteria developed to assist the team in testing and evaluating potential solutions?

<--- Score

125. What should a proof of concept or pilot accomplish?

<--- Score

126. What attendant changes will need to be made to ensure that the solution is successful?

<--- Score

127. Who controls the risk?
<--- Score

128. How will you recognize and celebrate results?
<--- Score

129. How scalable is your risk ownership solution?
<--- Score

130. Is risk ownership documentation maintained?
<--- Score

131. Is supporting risk ownership documentation required?
<--- Score

132. What were the underlying assumptions on the cost-benefit analysis?
<--- Score

133. How do you define the solutions' scope?
<--- Score

134. What risk ownership improvements can be made?
<--- Score

135. Is the risk ownership documentation thorough?
<--- Score

136. Where do the risk ownership decisions reside?
<--- Score

137. When you map the key players in your own work and the types/domains of relationships with them, which relationships do you find easy and which

challenging, and why?
<--- Score

138. Is any risk ownership documentation required?
<--- Score

139. Is there a small-scale pilot for proposed improvement(s)? What conclusions were drawn from the outcomes of a pilot?
<--- Score

140. What can you do to improve?
<--- Score

141. Who are the key stakeholders for the risk ownership evaluation?
<--- Score

142. How can you improve performance?
<--- Score

Add up total points for this section:
_ _ _ _ _ = Total points for this section

Divided by: _ _ _ _ _ _ (number of statements answered) = _ _ _ _ _ _
Average score for this section

Transfer your score to the risk ownership Index at the beginning of the Self-Assessment.

CRITERION #6: CONTROL:

INTENT: Implement the practical solution. Maintain the performance and correct possible complications.

In my belief, the answer to this question is clearly defined:

5 Strongly Agree

4 Agree

3 Neutral

2 Disagree

1 Strongly Disagree

1. What should you measure to verify efficiency gains?
<--- Score

2. How do you plan on providing proper recognition and disclosure of supporting companies?
<--- Score

3. Has the improved process and its steps been standardized?

<--- Score

4. What can you control?
<--- Score

5. Will any special training be provided for results interpretation?
<--- Score

6. How likely is the current risk ownership plan to come in on schedule or on budget?
<--- Score

7. How will input, process, and output variables be checked to detect for sub-optimal conditions?
<--- Score

8. Is there a control plan in place for sustaining improvements (short and long-term)?
<--- Score

9. What other areas of the group might benefit from the risk ownership team's improvements, knowledge, and learning?
<--- Score

10. What is your plan to assess your security risks?
<--- Score

11. Is new knowledge gained imbedded in the response plan?
<--- Score

12. How do you plan for the cost of succession?
<--- Score

13. What is the control/monitoring plan?
<--- Score

14. Does the risk ownership performance meet the customer's requirements?
<--- Score

15. What risk ownership standards are applicable?
<--- Score

16. Who is going to spread your message?
<--- Score

17. What is the recommended frequency of auditing?
<--- Score

18. Does a troubleshooting guide exist or is it needed?
<--- Score

19. Is reporting being used or needed?
<--- Score

20. Does the response plan contain a definite closed loop continual improvement scheme (e.g., plan-do-check-act)?
<--- Score

21. Are the planned controls working?
<--- Score

22. Is there a documented and implemented monitoring plan?
<--- Score

23. Is a response plan established and deployed?
<--- Score

24. Act/Adjust: What Do you Need to Do Differently?
<--- Score

25. How can you best use all of your knowledge repositories to enhance learning and sharing?
<--- Score

26. What do you measure to verify effectiveness gains?
<--- Score

27. Do you monitor the effectiveness of your risk ownership activities?
<--- Score

28. How do controls support value?
<--- Score

29. How is change control managed?
<--- Score

30. What other systems, operations, processes, and infrastructures (hiring practices, staffing, training, incentives/rewards, metrics/dashboards/scorecards, etc.) need updates, additions, changes, or deletions in order to facilitate knowledge transfer and improvements?
<--- Score

31. Is knowledge gained on process shared and institutionalized?
<--- Score

32. What adjustments to the strategies are needed?

<--- Score

33. Are operating procedures consistent?
<--- Score

34. How will report readings be checked to effectively monitor performance?
<--- Score

35. How do you encourage people to take control and responsibility?
<--- Score

36. Are suggested corrective/restorative actions indicated on the response plan for known causes to problems that might surface?
<--- Score

37. What key inputs and outputs are being measured on an ongoing basis?
<--- Score

38. Are new process steps, standards, and documentation ingrained into normal operations?
<--- Score

39. How do you monitor usage and cost?
<--- Score

40. Are you measuring, monitoring and predicting risk ownership activities to optimize operations and profitability, and enhancing outcomes?
<--- Score

41. Do you monitor the risk ownership decisions made and fine tune them as they evolve?

<--- Score

42. Where do ideas that reach policy makers and planners as proposals for risk ownership strengthening and reform actually originate?
<--- Score

43. Are the planned controls in place?
<--- Score

44. Who controls critical resources?
<--- Score

45. Will existing staff require re-training, for example, to learn new business processes?
<--- Score

46. Is there a risk ownership Communication plan covering who needs to get what information when?
<--- Score

47. How will new or emerging customer needs/ requirements be checked/communicated to orient the process toward meeting the new specifications and continually reducing variation?
<--- Score

48. Are there documented procedures?
<--- Score

49. Are the risk ownership standards challenging?
<--- Score

50. Is a response plan in place for when the input, process, or output measures indicate an 'out-of-control' condition?

<--- Score

51. What do your reports reflect?
<--- Score

52. In the case of a risk ownership project, the criteria for the audit derive from implementation objectives, an audit of a risk ownership project involves assessing whether the recommendations outlined for implementation have been met, can you track that any risk ownership project is implemented as planned, and is it working?
<--- Score

53. Can support from partners be adjusted?
<--- Score

54. Is there a recommended audit plan for routine surveillance inspections of risk ownership's gains?
<--- Score

55. Who has control over resources?
<--- Score

56. How will the process owner verify improvement in present and future sigma levels, process capabilities?
<--- Score

57. How will the day-to-day responsibilities for monitoring and continual improvement be transferred from the improvement team to the process owner?
<--- Score

58. How do your controls stack up?
<--- Score

59. What are you attempting to measure/monitor?
<--- Score

60. What is the best design framework for risk ownership organization now that, in a post industrial-age if the top-down, command and control model is no longer relevant?
<--- Score

61. Is there documentation that will support the successful operation of the improvement?
<--- Score

62. Are controls in place and consistently applied?
<--- Score

63. Who is the risk ownership process owner?
<--- Score

64. Will the team be available to assist members in planning investigations?
<--- Score

65. Is there a standardized process?
<--- Score

66. How widespread is its use?
<--- Score

67. How might the group capture best practices and lessons learned so as to leverage improvements?
<--- Score

68. Have new or revised work instructions resulted?
<--- Score

69. Has the risk ownership value of standards been quantified?

<--- Score

70. What are the known security controls?

<--- Score

71. Can you adapt and adjust to changing risk ownership situations?

<--- Score

72. What is your theory of human motivation, and how does your compensation plan fit with that view?

<--- Score

73. What should the next improvement project be that is related to risk ownership?

<--- Score

74. What quality tools were useful in the control phase?

<--- Score

75. Who will be in control?

<--- Score

76. How do you select, collect, align, and integrate risk ownership data and information for tracking daily operations and overall organizational performance, including progress relative to strategic objectives and action plans?

<--- Score

77. What are the critical parameters to watch?

<--- Score

78. How will the process owner and team be able to hold the gains?
<--- Score

79. Will your goals reflect your program budget?
<--- Score

80. Against what alternative is success being measured?
<--- Score

81. You may have created your quality measures at a time when you lacked resources, technology wasn't up to the required standard, or low service levels were the industry norm. Have those circumstances changed?
<--- Score

82. Do the risk ownership decisions you make today help people and the planet tomorrow?
<--- Score

83. How do senior leaders actions reflect a commitment to the organizations risk ownership values?
<--- Score

84. How do you establish and deploy modified action plans if circumstances require a shift in plans and rapid execution of new plans?
<--- Score

85. What are your results for key measures or indicators of the accomplishment of your risk

ownership strategy and action plans, including building and strengthening core competencies?
<--- Score

86. Is there a transfer of ownership and knowledge to process owner and process team tasked with the responsibilities.
<--- Score

87. Are documented procedures clear and easy to follow for the operators?
<--- Score

88. How is risk ownership project cost planned, managed, monitored?
<--- Score

89. What do you stand for--and what are you against?
<--- Score

90. What are customers monitoring?
<--- Score

91. Does job training on the documented procedures need to be part of the process team's education and training?
<--- Score

92. What are the key elements of your risk ownership performance improvement system, including your evaluation, organizational learning, and innovation processes?
<--- Score

93. How will risk ownership decisions be made and monitored?

<--- Score

94. Is there an action plan in case of emergencies?
<--- Score

Add up total points for this section:
_____ = Total points for this section

Divided by: _____ (number of
statements answered) = _____
Average score for this section

Transfer your score to the risk
ownership Index at the beginning of the
Self-Assessment.

CRITERION #7: SUSTAIN:

INTENT: Retain the benefits.

In my belief, the answer to this question is clearly defined:

5 Strongly Agree

4 Agree

3 Neutral

2 Disagree

1 Strongly Disagree

1. Who have you, as a company, historically been when you've been at your best?
<--- Score

2. How will you ensure you get what you expected?
<--- Score

3. What is your formula for success in risk ownership ?
<--- Score

4. How do you engage the workforce, in addition to satisfying them?
<--- Score

5. What happens at your organization when people fail?
<--- Score

6. Are you maintaining a past–present–future perspective throughout the risk ownership discussion?
<--- Score

7. What role does communication play in the success or failure of a risk ownership project?
<--- Score

8. Why is it important to have senior management support for a risk ownership project?
<--- Score

9. What are your most important goals for the strategic risk ownership objectives?
<--- Score

10. How can you become the company that would put you out of business?
<--- Score

11. Are you making progress, and are you making progress as risk ownership leaders?
<--- Score

12. Do you think you know, or do you know you know ?
<--- Score

13. Why not do risk ownership?
<--- Score

14. Who will determine interim and final deadlines?
<--- Score

15. What are you challenging?
<--- Score

16. Are the assumptions believable and achievable?
<--- Score

17. Who is on the team?
<--- Score

18. If you weren't already in this business, would you enter it today? And if not, what are you going to do about it?
<--- Score

19. How do you transition from the baseline to the target?
<--- Score

20. Are all key stakeholders present at all Structured Walkthroughs?
<--- Score

21. What are the challenges?
<--- Score

22. How do you determine the key elements that affect risk ownership workforce satisfaction, how are these elements determined for different workforce

groups and segments?
<--- Score

23. Where can you break convention?
<--- Score

24. What are current risk ownership paradigms?
<--- Score

25. How do you listen to customers to obtain actionable information?
<--- Score

26. Who, on the executive team or the board, has spoken to a customer recently?
<--- Score

27. Is there any reason to believe the opposite of my current belief?
<--- Score

28. Who do you think the world wants your organization to be?
<--- Score

29. How do you track customer value, profitability or financial return, organizational success, and sustainability?
<--- Score

30. Who will manage the integration of tools?
<--- Score

31. What is a feasible sequencing of reform initiatives over time?
<--- Score

32. Which individuals, teams or departments will be involved in risk ownership?
<--- Score

33. What are the gaps in your knowledge and experience?
<--- Score

34. What is your question? Why?
<--- Score

35. How do you ensure that implementations of risk ownership products are done in a way that ensures safety?
<--- Score

36. What is the purpose of risk ownership in relation to the mission?
<--- Score

37. What are the long-term risk ownership goals?
<--- Score

38. What happens when a new employee joins the organization?
<--- Score

39. Can you maintain your growth without detracting from the factors that have contributed to your success?
<--- Score

40. What is the recommended frequency of auditing?
<--- Score

41. Do you feel that more should be done in the risk ownership area?
<--- Score

42. What knowledge, skills and characteristics mark a good risk ownership project manager?
<--- Score

43. How do you foster the skills, knowledge, talents, attributes, and characteristics you want to have?
<--- Score

44. What unique value proposition (UVP) do you offer?
<--- Score

45. How do you accomplish your long range risk ownership goals?
<--- Score

46. Do you have an implicit bias for capital investments over people investments?
<--- Score

47. Do you have the right capabilities and capacities?
<--- Score

48. Why do and why don't your customers like your organization?
<--- Score

49. How do you maintain risk ownership's Integrity?
<--- Score

50. What information is critical to your organization that your executives are ignoring?

<--- Score

51. Who are four people whose careers you have enhanced?
<--- Score

52. When information truly is ubiquitous, when reach and connectivity are completely global, when computing resources are infinite, and when a whole new set of impossibilities are not only possible, but happening, what will that do to your business?
<--- Score

53. How are you doing compared to your industry?
<--- Score

54. Who will provide the final approval of risk ownership deliverables?
<--- Score

55. Who do we want your customers to become?
<--- Score

56. What will be the consequences to the stakeholder (financial, reputation etc) if risk ownership does not go ahead or fails to deliver the objectives?
<--- Score

57. What is your risk ownership strategy?
<--- Score

58. Do you think risk ownership accomplishes the goals you expect it to accomplish?
<--- Score

59. If you had to rebuild your organization without

any traditional competitive advantages (i.e., no killer technology, promising research, innovative product/ service delivery model, etcetera), how would your people have to approach their work and collaborate together in order to create the necessary conditions for success?
<--- Score

60. What is your competitive advantage?
<--- Score

61. What does your signature ensure?
<--- Score

62. What management system can you use to leverage the risk ownership experience, ideas, and concerns of the people closest to the work to be done?
<--- Score

63. What is your BATNA (best alternative to a negotiated agreement)?
<--- Score

64. How do you know if you are successful?
<--- Score

65. What is the estimated value of the project?
<--- Score

66. How important is risk ownership to the user organizations mission?
<--- Score

67. What are the barriers to increased risk ownership production?

<--- Score

68. What would have to be true for the option on the table to be the best possible choice?
<--- Score

69. How do you lead with risk ownership in mind?
<--- Score

70. What is effective risk ownership?
<--- Score

71. What must you excel at?
<--- Score

72. What are you trying to prove to yourself, and how might it be hijacking your life and business success?
<--- Score

73. If you do not follow, then how to lead?
<--- Score

74. What is the range of capabilities?
<--- Score

75. If you find that you havent accomplished one of the goals for one of the steps of the risk ownership strategy, what will you do to fix it?
<--- Score

76. What is the overall business strategy?
<--- Score

77. What should you stop doing?
<--- Score

78. Do you have enough freaky customers in your portfolio pushing you to the limit day in and day out?

<--- Score

79. If your customer were your grandmother, would you tell her to buy what you're selling?

<--- Score

80. Whom among your colleagues do you trust, and for what?

<--- Score

81. Is the risk ownership organization completing tasks effectively and efficiently?

<--- Score

82. What are specific risk ownership rules to follow?

<--- Score

83. What happens if you do not have enough funding?

<--- Score

84. How do you go about securing risk ownership?

<--- Score

85. What trophy do you want on your mantle?

<--- Score

86. What business benefits will risk ownership goals deliver if achieved?

<--- Score

87. Can you do all this work?

<--- Score

88. Who is the main stakeholder, with ultimate responsibility for driving risk ownership forward?
<--- Score

89. Who is responsible for ensuring appropriate resources (time, people and money) are allocated to risk ownership?
<--- Score

90. How do you govern and fulfill your societal responsibilities?
<--- Score

91. What potential megatrends could make your business model obsolete?
<--- Score

92. If no one would ever find out about your accomplishments, how would you lead differently?
<--- Score

93. How is implementation research currently incorporated into each of your goals?
<--- Score

94. In a project to restructure risk ownership outcomes, which stakeholders would you involve?
<--- Score

95. What relationships among risk ownership trends do you perceive?
<--- Score

96. What is the funding source for this project?
<--- Score

97. How do senior leaders deploy your organizations vision and values through your leadership system, to the workforce, to key suppliers and partners, and to customers and other stakeholders, as appropriate?
<--- Score

98. How likely is it that a customer would recommend your company to a friend or colleague?
<--- Score

99. Are you / should you be revolutionary or evolutionary?
<--- Score

100. If your company went out of business tomorrow, would anyone who doesn't get a paycheck here care?
<--- Score

101. What is the craziest thing you can do?
<--- Score

102. If you got fired and a new hire took your place, what would she do different?
<--- Score

103. What trouble can you get into?
<--- Score

104. If there were zero limitations, what would you do differently?
<--- Score

105. What new services of functionality will be implemented next with risk ownership ?

<--- Score

106. What are the short and long-term risk ownership goals?
<--- Score

107. What are the success criteria that will indicate that risk ownership objectives have been met and the benefits delivered?
<--- Score

108. How do you keep the momentum going?
<--- Score

109. What is the kind of project structure that would be appropriate for your risk ownership project, should it be formal and complex, or can it be less formal and relatively simple?
<--- Score

110. Who are your customers?
<--- Score

111. To whom do you add value?
<--- Score

112. Will it be accepted by users?
<--- Score

113. How will you know that the risk ownership project has been successful?
<--- Score

114. Is maximizing risk ownership protection the same as minimizing risk ownership loss?
<--- Score

115. Do you say no to customers for no reason?
<--- Score

116. What are strategies for increasing support and reducing opposition?
<--- Score

117. Which risk ownership goals are the most important?
<--- Score

118. How do you foster innovation?
<--- Score

119. Marketing budgets are tighter, consumers are more skeptical, and social media has changed forever the way we talk about risk ownership, how do you gain traction?
<--- Score

120. Who is responsible for risk ownership?
<--- Score

121. Do you have past risk ownership successes?
<--- Score

122. How do you provide a safe environment -physically and emotionally?
<--- Score

123. What are the rules and assumptions your industry operates under? What if the opposite were true?
<--- Score

124. Are you using a design thinking approach and

integrating Innovation, risk ownership Experience, and Brand Value?
<--- Score

125. What one word do you want to own in the minds of your customers, employees, and partners?
<--- Score

126. Is it economical; do you have the time and money?
<--- Score

127. What have been your experiences in defining long range risk ownership goals?
<--- Score

128. How do you stay inspired?
<--- Score

129. Is there a work around that you can use?
<--- Score

130. How much does risk ownership help?
<--- Score

131. How do you create buy-in?
<--- Score

132. Political -is anyone trying to undermine this project?
<--- Score

133. How do you proactively clarify deliverables and risk ownership quality expectations?
<--- Score

134. How can you negotiate risk ownership successfully with a stubborn boss, an irate client, or a deceitful coworker?

<--- Score

135. What you are going to do to affect the numbers?

<--- Score

136. In retrospect, of the projects that you pulled the plug on, what percent do you wish had been allowed to keep going, and what percent do you wish had ended earlier?

<--- Score

137. How much contingency will be available in the budget?

<--- Score

138. Is risk ownership realistic, or are you setting yourself up for failure?

<--- Score

139. Operational - will it work?

<--- Score

140. What are your personal philosophies regarding risk ownership and how do they influence your work?

<--- Score

141. What could happen if you do not do it?

<--- Score

142. Are assumptions made in risk ownership stated explicitly?

<--- Score

143. How do you deal with risk ownership changes?

<--- Score

144. Who do you want your customers to become?

<--- Score

145. Are you satisfied with your current role? If not, what is missing from it?

<--- Score

146. What goals did you miss?

<--- Score

147. Is a risk ownership team work effort in place?

<--- Score

148. What risk ownership skills are most important?

<--- Score

149. Do you know what you are doing? And who do you call if you don't?

<--- Score

150. Would you rather sell to knowledgeable and informed customers or to uninformed customers?

<--- Score

151. Who are the key stakeholders?

<--- Score

152. What is the source of the strategies for risk ownership strengthening and reform?

<--- Score

153. What was the last experiment you ran?

<--- Score

154. Which models, tools and techniques are necessary?

<--- Score

155. What are the key enablers to make this risk ownership move?

<--- Score

156. Who will be responsible for deciding whether risk ownership goes ahead or not after the initial investigations?

<--- Score

157. What projects are going on in the organization today, and what resources are those projects using from the resource pools?

<--- Score

158. How will you insure seamless interoperability of risk ownership moving forward?

<--- Score

159. Who uses your product in ways you never expected?

<--- Score

160. How will you motivate the stakeholders with the least vested interest?

<--- Score

161. Whose voice (department, ethnic group, women, older workers, etc) might you have missed hearing from in your company, and how might you amplify

this voice to create positive momentum for your business?

<--- Score

162. How do you make it meaningful in connecting risk ownership with what users do day-to-day?

<--- Score

163. What may be the consequences for the performance of an organization if all stakeholders are not consulted regarding risk ownership?

<--- Score

164. Is your basic point _____ or _____?

<--- Score

165. Do you see more potential in people than they do in themselves?

<--- Score

166. Why will customers want to buy your organizations products/services?

<--- Score

167. Will there be any necessary staff changes (redundancies or new hires)?

<--- Score

168. What is an unauthorized commitment?

<--- Score

169. If you were responsible for initiating and implementing major changes in your organization, what steps might you take to ensure acceptance of those changes?

<--- Score

170. What stupid rule would you most like to kill?
<--- Score

171. Who is responsible for errors?
<--- Score

172. What are the performance and scale of the risk ownership tools?
<--- Score

173. What are the essentials of internal risk ownership management?
<--- Score

174. Can the schedule be done in the given time?
<--- Score

175. In the past year, what have you done (or could you have done) to increase the accurate perception of your company/brand as ethical and honest?
<--- Score

176. What did you miss in the interview for the worst hire you ever made?
<--- Score

177. Do you have the right people on the bus?
<--- Score

178. Are the criteria for selecting recommendations stated?
<--- Score

179. How can you become more high-tech but still be

high touch?

<--- Score

180. How do you set risk ownership stretch targets and how do you get people to not only participate in setting these stretch targets but also that they strive to achieve these?

<--- Score

181. How can you incorporate support to ensure safe and effective use of risk ownership into the services that you provide?

<--- Score

182. Is there any existing risk ownership governance structure?

<--- Score

183. Instead of going to current contacts for new ideas, what if you reconnected with dormant contacts--the people you used to know? If you were going reactivate a dormant tie, who would it be?

<--- Score

184. What are internal and external risk ownership relations?

<--- Score

185. What is it like to work for you?

<--- Score

186. Ask yourself: how would you do this work if you only had one staff member to do it?

<--- Score

187. How do you manage risk ownership Knowledge Management (KM)?
<--- Score

188. How long will it take to change?
<--- Score

189. What are the business goals risk ownership is aiming to achieve?
<--- Score

190. Did your employees make progress today?
<--- Score

191. Why should people listen to you?
<--- Score

192. What are the potential basics of risk ownership fraud?
<--- Score

Add up total points for this section:
_ _ _ _ _ = Total points for this section

Divided by: _ _ _ _ _ _ (number of statements answered) = _ _ _ _ _ _
Average score for this section

Transfer your score to the risk ownership Index at the beginning of the Self-Assessment.

Risk Ownership and Managing Projects, Criteria for Project Managers:

1.0 Initiating Process Group: Risk Ownership

1. Are stakeholders properly informed about the status of the Risk Ownership project?

2. How can you make your needs known?

3. What do you need to do?

4. What were things that you did very well and want to do the same again on the next Risk Ownership project?

5. What communication items need improvement?

6. Do you know if the Risk Ownership project requires outside equipment or vendor resources?

7. Contingency planning. if a risk event occurs, what will you do?

8. What are the short and long term implications?

9. What were things that you did well, and could improve, and how?

10. What are the pressing issues of the hour?

11. What were things that you need to improve?

12. What input will you be required to provide the Risk Ownership project team?

13. What are the required resources?

14. Does the Risk Ownership project team have enough people to execute the Risk Ownership project plan?

15. Who is behind the Risk Ownership project?

16. The Risk Ownership project you are managing has nine stakeholders. How many channel of communications are there between corresponding stakeholders?

17. How will it affect me?

18. Are you just doing busywork to pass the time?

19. Who is performing the work of the Risk Ownership project?

20. Were resources available as planned?

1.1 Project Charter: Risk Ownership

21. Why the improvements?

22. What are the constraints?

23. What are the assigned resources?

24. Dependent Risk Ownership projects: what Risk Ownership projects must be underway or completed before this Risk Ownership project can be successful?

25. Did your Risk Ownership project ask for this?

26. Pop quiz – which are the same inputs as in the Risk Ownership project charter?

27. What is the most common tool for helping define the detail?

28. What are the known stakeholder requirements?

29. What are some examples of a business case?

30. Run it as as a startup?

31. Must Have?

32. When will this occur?

33. What material?

34. What barriers do you predict to your success?

35. What is in it for you?

36. Why Outsource?

37. What goes into your Risk Ownership project Charter?

38. Why do you need to manage scope?

39. Who will take notes, document decisions?

40. When is a charter needed?

1.2 Stakeholder Register: Risk Ownership

41. What opportunities exist to provide communications?

42. How much influence do they have on the Risk Ownership project?

43. Who are the stakeholders?

44. Who wants to talk about Security?

45. What are the major Risk Ownership project milestones requiring communications or providing communications opportunities?

46. Is your organization ready for change?

47. What & Why?

48. How will reports be created?

49. What is the power of the stakeholder?

50. Who is managing stakeholder engagement?

51. How big is the gap?

52. How should employers make voices heard?

1.3 Stakeholder Analysis Matrix: Risk Ownership

53. How will the Risk Ownership project benefit them?

54. What do people from other organizations see as your organizations weaknesses?

55. Who is directly responsible for decisions on issues important to the Risk Ownership project?

56. What should thwe organizations stakeholders avoid?

57. Continuity, supply chain robustness?

58. What makes a person a stakeholder?

59. What do your organizations stakeholders do better than anyone else?

60. Alliances: with which other actors is the actor allied, how are they interconnected?

61. Supporters; who are the supporters?

62. Are you working on the right risks?

63. Who will promote/support the Risk Ownership project, provided that they are involved?

64. Identify the stakeholders levels most frequently used –or at least sought– in your Risk Ownership

projects and for which purpose?

65. What advantages do your organizations stakeholders have?

66. Where are mitigation costs factored in?

67. Technology development and innovation?

68. What mechanisms are proposed to monitor and measure Risk Ownership project performance in terms of social development outcomes?

69. How do customers express needs?

70. What organizational arrangements are planned to ensure the Risk Ownership project achieves its social development outcomes?

71. Who are potential allies and opponents?

72. Are there two or three that rise to the top, and a couple that are sliding to the bottom?

2.0 Planning Process Group: Risk Ownership

73. To what extent are the participating departments coordinating with each other?

74. How well do the team follow the chosen processes?

75. What are the different approaches to building the WBS?

76. What input will you be required to provide the Risk Ownership project team?

77. You are creating your WBS and find that you keep decomposing tasks into smaller and smaller units. How can you tell when you are done?

78. Does the program have follow-up mechanisms (to verify the quality of the products, punctuality of delivery, etc.) to measure progress in the achievement of the envisaged results?

79. How many days can task X be late in starting without affecting the Risk Ownership project completion date?

80. Are there efficient coordination mechanisms to avoid overloading the counterparts, participating stakeholders?

81. Product breakdown structure (pbs): what is the

Risk Ownership project result or product, and how should it look like, what are its parts?

82. What is involved in Risk Ownership project scope management, and why is good Risk Ownership project scope management so important on information technology Risk Ownership projects?

83. Professionals want to know what is expected from them; what are the deliverables?

84. How well will the chosen processes produce the expected results?

85. Have more efficient (sensitive) and appropriate measures been adopted to respond to the political and socio-cultural problems identified?

86. To what extent has a PMO contributed to raising the quality of the design of the Risk Ownership project?

87. What is the critical path for this Risk Ownership project, and what is the duration of the critical path?

88. Mitigate. what will you do to minimize the impact should a risk event occur?

89. To what extent have public/private national resources and/or counterparts been mobilized to contribute to the programs objective and produce results and impacts?

90. What will you do to minimize the impact should a risk event occur?

91. Does it make any difference if you are successful?

2.1 Project Management Plan: Risk Ownership

92. Was the peer (technical) review of the cost estimates duly coordinated with the cost estimate center of expertise and addressed in the review documentation and certification?

93. Why Change?

94. Will you add a schedule and diagram?

95. What is Risk Ownership project scope management?

96. How do you manage integration?

97. Does the implementation plan have an appropriate division of responsibilities?

98. What worked well?

99. What data/reports/tools/etc. do your PMs need?

100. Are there any windfall benefits that would accrue to the Risk Ownership project sponsor or other parties?

101. What are the assumptions?

102. Does the selected plan protect privacy?

103. What data/reports/tools/etc. do program

managers need?

104. Is there an incremental analysis/cost effectiveness analysis of proposed mitigation features based on an approved method and using an accepted model?

105. What is risk management?

106. What should you drop in order to add something new?

107. Is there anything you would now do differently on your Risk Ownership project based on past experience?

108. What went right?

2.2 Scope Management Plan: Risk Ownership

109. Can the Risk Ownership project team do several activities in parallel?

110. How do you plan to control Scope Creep?

111. Time estimation – how much time will be needed?

112. Are you meeting with stake holders and team members?

113. Are agendas created for each meeting with meeting objectives, meeting topics, invitee list, and action items from past meetings?

114. Are staff skills known and available for each task?

115. Are schedule deliverables actually delivered?

116. Describe how the deliverables will be verified against the Risk Ownership project scope. To whom will the deliverables be first presented for inspection and verification?

117. Are decisions captured in a decisions log?

118. Are calculations and results of analyzes essentially correct?

119. How relevant is this attribute to this Risk

Ownership project or audit?

120. What does the critical path really mean?

121. Is there a scope management plan that includes how Risk Ownership project scope will be defined, developed, monitored, validated and controlled?

122. Have all involved Risk Ownership project stakeholders and work groups committed to the Risk Ownership project?

123. What if you do not have more detailed information on the report?

124. Are the quality tools and methods identified in the Quality Plan appropriate to the Risk Ownership project?

125. Is the assigned Risk Ownership project manager a PMP (Certified Risk Ownership project manager) and experienced?

126. Is there an approved case?

127. Is there a set of procedures defining the scope, procedures, and deliverables defining quality control?

128. Is there a formal process for updating the Risk Ownership project baseline?

2.3 Requirements Management Plan: Risk Ownership

129. Should you include sub-activities?

130. To see if a requirement statement is sufficiently well-defined, read it from the developers perspective. Mentally add the phrase, call me when youre done to the end of the requirement and see if that makes you nervous. In other words, would you need additional clarification from the author to understand the requirement well enough to design and implement it?

131. Will the product release be stable and mature enough to be deployed in the user community?

132. Have stakeholders been instructed in the Change Control process?

133. Are actual resource expenditures versus planned still acceptable?

134. Subject to change control?

135. The wbs is developed as part of a joint planning session. and how do you know that youhave done this right?

136. Do you know which stakeholders will participate in the requirements effort?

137. Is the user satisfied?

138. How will the information be distributed?

139. When and how will a requirements baseline be established in this Risk Ownership project?

140. How often will the reporting occur?

141. What performance metrics will be used?

142. Who is responsible for monitoring and tracking the Risk Ownership project requirements?

143. Do you have price sheets and a methodology for determining the total proposal cost?

144. Is the system software (non-operating system) new to the IT Risk Ownership project team?

145. Did you avoid subjective, flowery or non-specific statements?

146. How will you develop the schedule of requirements activities?

147. Did you use declarative statements?

148. What information regarding the Risk Ownership project requirements will be reported?

2.4 Requirements Documentation: Risk Ownership

149. How will they be documented / shared?

150. Are there legal issues?

151. How to document system requirements?

152. What kind of entity is a problem ?

153. Who provides requirements?

154. What is your Elevator Speech?

155. What is the risk associated with the technology?

156. Who is involved?

157. What is a show stopper in the requirements?

158. How can you document system requirements?

159. Who is interacting with the system?

160. Is the requirement realistically testable?

161. Basic work/business process; high-level, what is being touched?

162. Is new technology needed?

163. What will be the integration problems?

164. Can you check system requirements?

165. How will the proposed Risk Ownership project help?

166. What are current process problems?

167. What is the risk associated with cost and schedule?

168. How does what is being described meet the business need?

2.5 Requirements Traceability Matrix: Risk Ownership

169. What are the chronologies, contingencies, consequences, criteria?

170. Is there a requirements traceability process in place?

171. Why use a WBS?

172. Do you have a clear understanding of all subcontracts in place?

173. Describe the process for approving requirements so they can be added to the traceability matrix and Risk Ownership project work can be performed. Will the Risk Ownership project requirements become approved in writing?

174. How will it affect the stakeholders personally in career?

175. How small is small enough?

176. Why do you manage scope?

177. How do you manage scope?

178. What percentage of Risk Ownership projects are producing traceability matrices between requirements and other work products?

179. Will you use a Requirements Traceability Matrix?

180. What is the WBS?

2.6 Project Scope Statement: Risk Ownership

181. Is the Risk Ownership project manager qualified and experienced in Risk Ownership project management?

182. Has everyone approved the Risk Ownership projects scope statement?

183. Was planning completed before the Risk Ownership project was initiated?

184. Elements of scope management that deal with concept development ?

185. Change management vs. change leadership - what is the difference?

186. Once its defined, what is the stability of the Risk Ownership project scope?

187. Is the Risk Ownership project sponsor function identified and defined?

188. Do you anticipate new stakeholders joining the Risk Ownership project over time?

189. Is there a Quality Assurance Plan documented and filed?

190. How will you verify the accuracy of the work of the Risk Ownership project, and what constitutes

acceptance of the deliverables?

191. What is a process you might recommend to verify the accuracy of the research deliverable?

192. Is this process communicated to the customer and team members?

193. Is the scope of your Risk Ownership project well defined?

194. What is change?

195. Are there completion/verification criteria defined for each task producing an output?

196. What is the product of this Risk Ownership project?

197. Is there a baseline plan against which to measure progress?

198. Any new risks introduced or old risks impacted. Are there issues that could affect the existing requirements for the result, service, or product if the scope changes?

2.7 Assumption and Constraint Log: Risk Ownership

199. Does the Risk Ownership project have a formal Risk Ownership project Plan?

200. Does the plan conform to standards?

201. Are there processes defining how software will be developed including development methods, overall timeline for development, software product standards, and traceability?

202. What threats might prevent you from getting there?

203. Can you perform this task or activity in a more effective manner?

204. Does the document/deliverable meet general requirements (for example, statement of work) for all deliverables?

205. Does a documented Risk Ownership project organizational policy & plan (i.e. governance model) exist?

206. Contradictory information between document sections?

207. How do you design an auditing system?

208. Have the scope, objectives, costs, benefits and

impacts been communicated to all involved and/or impacted stakeholders and work groups?

209. No superfluous information or marketing narrative?

210. Violation trace: why ?

211. Is this process still needed?

212. Are funding and staffing resource estimates sufficiently detailed and documented for use in planning and tracking the Risk Ownership project?

213. Is staff trained on the software technologies that are being used on the Risk Ownership project?

214. How relevant is this attribute to this Risk Ownership project or audit?

215. Do you know what your customers expectations are regarding this process?

216. What other teams / processes would be impacted by changes to the current process, and how?

217. Model-building: what data-analytic strategies are useful when building proportional-hazards models?

2.8 Work Breakdown Structure: Risk Ownership

218. Is the work breakdown structure (wbs) defined and is the scope of the Risk Ownership project clear with assigned deliverable owners?

219. Where does it take place?

220. When does it have to be done?

221. When would you develop a Work Breakdown Structure?

222. Can you make it?

223. How will you and your Risk Ownership project team define the Risk Ownership projects scope and work breakdown structure?

224. How many levels?

225. How big is a work-package?

226. What has to be done?

227. Do you need another level?

228. Is it a change in scope?

229. How much detail?

230. What is the probability that the Risk Ownership

project duration will exceed xx weeks?

231. How far down?

232. Who has to do it?

233. What is the probability of completing the Risk Ownership project in less that xx days?

234. When do you stop?

235. Is it still viable?

2.9 WBS Dictionary: Risk Ownership

236. Budgeted cost for work performed?

237. Are Risk Ownership projected overhead costs in each pool and the associated direct costs used as the basis for establishing interim rates for allocating overhead to contracts?

238. Do work packages consist of discrete tasks which are adequately described?

239. Is all budget available as management reserve identified and excluded from the performance measurement baseline?

240. Are the overhead pools formally and adequately identified?

241. Is the anticipated (firm and potential) business base Risk Ownership projected in a rational, consistent manner?

242. Are estimates of costs at completion generated in a rational, consistent manner?

243. What is the goal?

244. Are detailed work packages planned as far in advance as practicable?

245. Is undistributed budget limited to contract effort which cannot yet be planned to CWBS elements at or below the level specified for reporting to the

Government?

246. Knowledgeable Risk Ownership projections of future performance?

247. Is cost performance measurement at the point in time most suitable for the category of material involved, and no earlier than the time of actual receipt of material?

248. Are procedures established to prevent changes to the contract budget base other than the already stated authorized by contractual action?

249. Are indirect costs charged to the appropriate indirect pools and incurring organization?

250. Where engineering standards or other internal work measurement systems are used, is there a formal relationship between corresponding values and work package budgets?

251. Are data elements summarized through the functional organizational structure for progressively higher levels of management?

252. Are internal budgets for authorized, and not priced changes based on the contractors resource plan for accomplishing the work?

253. Is work progressively subdivided into detailed work packages as requirements are defined?

254. Are overhead budgets and costs being handled according to the disclosure statement when applicable, or otherwise properly classified (for

example, engineering overhead, IR&D)?

2.10 Schedule Management Plan: Risk Ownership

255. Is documentation created for communication with the suppliers and Vendors?

256. Are the constraints or deadlines associated with the task accurate?

257. Is the correct WBS element identified for each task and milestone in the IMS?

258. Have reserves been created to address risks?

259. Are tasks tracked by hours?

260. Has a Risk Ownership project Communications Plan been developed?

261. Are risk oriented checklists used during risk identification?

262. Is there an on-going process in place to monitor Risk Ownership project risks?

263. Are the quality tools and methods identified in the Quality Plan appropriate to the Risk Ownership project?

264. Is an industry recognized mechanized support tool(s) being used for Risk Ownership project scheduling & tracking?

265. Are risk triggers captured?

266. Are the appropriate IT resources adequate to meet planned commitments?

267. Has a quality assurance plan been developed for the Risk Ownership project?

268. Are mitigation strategies identified?

269. Have Risk Ownership project management standards and procedures been identified / established and documented?

270. Are cause and effect determined for risks when they occur?

271. Does the schedule have reasonable float?

272. Is it standard practice to formally commit stakeholders to the Risk Ownership project via agreements?

273. Is there a formal process for updating the Risk Ownership project baseline?

274. Which status reports are received per the Risk Ownership project Plan?

2.11 Activity List: Risk Ownership

275. When will the work be performed?

276. In what sequence?

277. What is your organizations history in doing similar activities?

278. For other activities, how much delay can be tolerated?

279. What is the probability the Risk Ownership project can be completed in xx weeks?

280. How can the Risk Ownership project be displayed graphically to better visualize the activities?

281. What are you counting on?

282. Who will perform the work?

283. What is the total time required to complete the Risk Ownership project if no delays occur?

284. Where will it be performed?

285. Can you determine the activity that must finish, before this activity can start?

286. What went well?

287. How do you determine the late start (LS) for each activity?

288. Are the required resources available or need to be acquired?

289. How much slack is available in the Risk Ownership project?

290. How detailed should a Risk Ownership project get?

291. How difficult will it be to do specific activities on this Risk Ownership project?

292. What is the LF and LS for each activity?

2.12 Activity Attributes: Risk Ownership

293. How difficult will it be to complete specific activities on this Risk Ownership project?

294. Are the required resources available?

295. Why?

296. What conclusions/generalizations can you draw from this?

297. Resources to accomplish the work?

298. How many days do you need to complete the work scope with a limit of X number of resources?

299. Were there other ways you could have organized the data to achieve similar results?

300. Activity: what is In the Bag?

301. Where else does it apply?

302. Have you identified the Activity Leveling Priority code value on each activity?

303. How many resources do you need to complete the work scope within a limit of X number of days?

304. Can you re-assign any activities to another resource to resolve an over-allocation?

305. Activity: fair or not fair?

306. Time for overtime?

307. Is there a trend during the year?

308. What activity do you think you should spend the most time on?

309. Activity: what is Missing?

310. Has management defined a definite timeframe for the turnaround or Risk Ownership project window?

311. What is missing?

312. Have constraints been applied to the start and finish milestones for the phases?

2.13 Milestone List: Risk Ownership

313. New USPs?

314. How difficult will it be to do specific activities on this Risk Ownership project?

315. What specific improvements did you make to the Risk Ownership project proposal since the previous time?

316. What background experience, skills, and strengths does the team bring to your organization?

317. Legislative effects?

318. Insurmountable weaknesses?

319. How soon can the activity finish?

320. How soon can the activity start?

321. Who will manage the Risk Ownership project on a day-to-day basis?

322. Vital contracts and partners?

323. Do you foresee any technical risks or developmental challenges?

324. How will the milestone be verified?

325. Loss of key staff?

326. Describe the concept of the technology, product or service that will be or has been developed. How will it be used?

327. Describe your organizations strengths and core competencies. What factors will make your organization succeed?

328. Own known vulnerabilities?

329. Sustaining internal capabilities?

330. It is to be a narrative text providing the crucial aspects of your Risk Ownership project proposal answering what, who, how, when and where?

331. Describe the industry you are in and the market growth opportunities. What is the market for your technology, product or service?

2.14 Network Diagram: Risk Ownership

332. What activity must be completed immediately before this activity can start?

333. What job or jobs could run concurrently?

334. Planning: who, how long, what to do?

335. How confident can you be in your milestone dates and the delivery date?

336. What to do and When?

337. Are the gantt chart and/or network diagram updated periodically and used to assess the overall Risk Ownership project timetable?

338. How difficult will it be to do specific activities on this Risk Ownership project?

339. If a current contract exists, can you provide the vendor name, contract start, and contract expiration date?

340. What job or jobs follow it?

341. If x is long, what would be the completion time if you break x into two parallel parts of y weeks and z weeks?

342. Exercise: what is the probability that the Risk

Ownership project duration will exceed xx weeks?

343. What controls the start and finish of a job?

344. Can you calculate the confidence level?

345. Review the logical flow of the network diagram. Take a look at which activities you have first and then sequence the activities. Do they make sense?

346. What job or jobs precede it?

347. Will crashing x weeks return more in benefits than it costs?

348. What must be completed before an activity can be started?

2.15 Activity Resource Requirements: Risk Ownership

349. Organizational Applicability?

350. Do you use tools like decomposition and rolling-wave planning to produce the activity list and other outputs?

351. Why do you do that?

352. How do you manage time?

353. Which logical relationship does the PDM use most often?

354. Is there anything planned that does not need to be here?

355. What is the Work Plan Standard?

356. How many signatures do you require on a check and does this match what is in your policy and procedures?

357. How do you handle petty cash?

358. What are constraints that you might find during the Human Resource Planning process?

359. When does monitoring begin?

360. Other support in specific areas?

361. Anything else?

362. Are there unresolved issues that need to be addressed?

2.16 Resource Breakdown Structure: Risk Ownership

363. Who will use the system?

364. What can you do to improve productivity?

365. Who will be used as a Risk Ownership project team member?

366. How can this help you with team building?

367. What is each stakeholders desired outcome for the Risk Ownership project?

368. What is the difference between % Complete and % work?

369. What is the number one predictor of a groups productivity?

370. What are the requirements for resource data?

371. Is predictive resource analysis being done?

372. How should the information be delivered?

373. What is the purpose of assigning and documenting responsibility?

374. Which resources should be in the resource pool?

375. The list could probably go on, but, the thing that

you would most like to know is, How long & How much?

376. What went wrong?

377. What is Risk Ownership project communication management?

378. Which resource planning tool provides information on resource responsibility and accountability?

379. What defines a successful Risk Ownership project?

380. Why is this important?

381. When do they need the information?

2.17 Activity Duration Estimates: Risk Ownership

382. Why is it difficult to use Risk Ownership project management software well?

383. What is the career outlook for Risk Ownership project managers in information technology?

384. Under corresponding circumstances what would be the best thing to do?

385. Does a process exist to identify individuals authorized to make certain decisions?

386. Where do schedules come from?

387. Which tips for taking the PMP exam do you think would be most helpful for you?

388. Are operational definitions created to identify quality measurement criteria for specific activities?

389. List five reasons why organizations outsource. Why is there a growing trend in outsourcing, especially in the government?

390. Mass, power, cost ... why not time?

391. Are measurement techniques employed to determine the potential impact of proposed changes?

392. After changes are approved are Risk Ownership

project documents updated and distributed?

393. What are the main types of goods and services being outsourced?

394. Are procurement documents used to solicit accurate and complete proposals from prospective sellers?

395. What type of contract was used and why?

396. Calculate the expected duration for an activity that has a most likely time of 5, a pessimistic time of 13, and a optimiztic time of 3?

397. Is the cost performance monitored to identify variances from the plan?

398. What is the duration of a milestone?

399. Does a process exist to determine the potential loss or gain if risk events occur?

400. Who will be the main sponsor for it?

401. Do you think Risk Ownership project managers of large information technology Risk Ownership projects need strong technical skills?

2.18 Duration Estimating Worksheet: Risk Ownership

402. When do the individual activities need to start and finish?

403. What is cost and Risk Ownership project cost management?

404. What info is needed?

405. Is the Risk Ownership project responsive to community need?

406. Science = process: remember the scientific method?

407. What is your role?

408. When, then?

409. Can the Risk Ownership project be constructed as planned?

410. What questions do you have?

411. Why estimate costs?

412. What are the critical bottleneck activities?

413. What is the total time required to complete the Risk Ownership project if no delays occur?

414. Small or large Risk Ownership project?

415. Will the Risk Ownership project collaborate with the local community and leverage resources?

416. When does your organization expect to be able to complete it?

417. Is a construction detail attached (to aid in explanation)?

418. What is next?

2.19 Project Schedule: Risk Ownership

419. Did the final product meet or exceed user expectations?

420. Why or why not?

421. How can you shorten the schedule?

422. Activity charts and bar charts are graphical representations of a Risk Ownership project schedule ...how do they differ?

423. Have all Risk Ownership project delays been adequately accounted for, communicated to all stakeholders and adjustments made in overall Risk Ownership project schedule?

424. Are the original Risk Ownership project schedule and budget realistic?

425. Is the Risk Ownership project schedule available for all Risk Ownership project team members to review?

426. Did the Risk Ownership project come in on schedule?

427. How do you know that youhave done this right?

428. Schedule/cost recovery?

429. If you can not fix it, how do you do it differently?

430. How much slack is available in the Risk Ownership project?

431. Did the Risk Ownership project come in under budget?

432. Understand the constraints used in preparing the schedule. Are activities connected because logic dictates the order in which others occur?

433. Does the condition or event threaten the Risk Ownership projects objectives in any ways?

434. Are there activities that came from a template or previous Risk Ownership project that are not applicable on this phase of this Risk Ownership project?

435. Why is this particularly bad?

436. Why do you need to manage Risk Ownership project Risk?

437. Are all remaining durations correct?

2.20 Cost Management Plan: Risk Ownership

438. Cost variances – how will cost variances be identified and corrected?

439. Have all unresolved risks been documented?

440. What would the life cycle costs be?

441. Are the key elements of a Risk Ownership project Charter present?

442. Has a quality assurance plan been developed for the Risk Ownership project?

443. Have all necessary approvals been obtained?

444. Were Risk Ownership project team members involved in detailed estimating and scheduling?

445. Has a Risk Ownership project Communications Plan been developed?

446. Sensitivity analysis?

447. Cost estimate preparation – What cost estimates will be prepared during the Risk Ownership project phases?

448. Are key risk mitigation strategies added to the Risk Ownership project schedule?

449. Is the steering committee active in Risk Ownership project oversight?

450. Is the Risk Ownership project schedule available for all Risk Ownership project team members to review?

451. Is there an onboarding process in place?

452. What is Risk Ownership project cost management?

453. What strengths do you have?

454. What is cost and Risk Ownership project cost management?

455. What will be the split of responsibilities of progress measurement and controls among the owner, contractor, subcontractors, and vendors?

2.21 Activity Cost Estimates: Risk Ownership

456. Maintenance Reserve?

457. How do you fund change orders?

458. Was it performed on time?

459. Will you need to provide essential services information about activities?

460. Did the consultant work with local staff to develop local capacity?

461. If you are asked to lower your estimate because the price is too high, what are your options?

462. Certification of actual expenditures?

463. How quickly can the task be done with the skills available?

464. What is Risk Ownership project cost management?

465. Does the estimator have experience?

466. Performance bond should always provide what part of the contract value?

467. How Award?

468. One way to define activities is to consider how organization employees describe jobs to families and friends. You basically want to know, What do you do?

469. Where can you get activity reports?

470. Does the estimator estimate by task or by person?

471. Who & what determines the need for contracted services?

472. What happens if you cannot produce the documentation for the single audit?

473. Would you hire them again?

2.22 Cost Estimating Worksheet: Risk Ownership

474. What additional Risk Ownership project(s) could be initiated as a result of this Risk Ownership project?

475. Is the Risk Ownership project responsive to community need?

476. What is the estimated labor cost today based upon this information?

477. What happens to any remaining funds not used?

478. Can a trend be established from historical performance data on the selected measure and are the criteria for using trend analysis or forecasting methods met?

479. What will others want?

480. What can be included?

481. Who is best positioned to know and assist in identifying corresponding factors?

482. What costs are to be estimated?

483. Will the Risk Ownership project collaborate with the local community and leverage resources?

484. How will the results be shared and to whom?

485. Value pocket identification & quantification what are value pockets?

486. Identify the timeframe necessary to monitor progress and collect data to determine how the selected measure has changed?

487. Ask: are others positioned to know, are others credible, and will others cooperate?

488. What is the purpose of estimating?

489. Does the Risk Ownership project provide innovative ways for stakeholders to overcome obstacles or deliver better outcomes?

490. Is it feasible to establish a control group arrangement?

2.23 Cost Baseline: Risk Ownership

491. How likely is it to go wrong?

492. Are there contingencies or conditions related to the acceptance?

493. When should cost estimates be developed?

494. Where do changes come from?

495. What is the reality?

496. How concrete were original objectives?

497. What is the most important thing to do next to make your Risk Ownership project successful?

498. Will the Risk Ownership project fail if the change request is not executed?

499. Is there anything you need from upper management in order to be successful?

500. Is the cr within Risk Ownership project scope?

501. Impact to environment?

502. Does a process exist for establishing a cost baseline to measure Risk Ownership project performance?

503. Definition of done can be traced back to the definitions of what are you providing to the customer

in terms of deliverables?

504. Does the suggested change request represent a desired enhancement to the products functionality?

505. What is it ?

506. Who will use corresponding metrics ?

507. What is the consequence?

508. Risk Ownership project goals -should others be reconsidered?

509. How do you manage cost?

510. Have all approved changes to the Risk Ownership project requirement been identified and impact on the performance, cost, and schedule baselines documented?

2.24 Quality Management Plan: Risk Ownership

511. Are there procedures in place to effectively manage interdependencies with other Risk Ownership projects / systems?

512. How does your organization maintain a safe and healthy work environment?

513. How do you measure?

514. What would you gain if you spent time working to improve this process?

515. How do your action plans support the strategic objectives?

516. Do you periodically review your data quality system to see that it is up to date and appropriate?

517. Have Risk Ownership project management standards and procedures been established and documented?

518. Who gets results of work?

519. How will you know that a change is actually an improvement?

520. What changes can you make that will result in improvement?

521. How are changes approved?

522. Are qmps good forever?

523. Do you keep back-up copies of any data?

524. Account for the procedures used to verify the data quality of the data being reviewed?

525. How are changes to procedures made?

526. You know what your customers expectations are regarding this process?

527. How do senior leaders review organizational performance?

528. Is there a Quality Management Plan?

529. What would be the next steps or what else should you do at this point?

530. With the five whys method, the team considers why the issue being explored occurred. do others then take that initial answer and ask why?

2.25 Quality Metrics: Risk Ownership

531. Was review conducted per standard protocols?

532. What metrics are important and most beneficial to measure?

533. What level of statistical confidence do you use?

534. What if the biggest risk to your business were the already stated people who do not complain?

535. There are many reasons to shore up quality-related metrics, and what metrics are important?

536. When will the Final Guidance will be issued?

537. Are applicable standards referenced and available?

538. Are interface issues coordinated?

539. Which report did you use to create the data you are submitting?

540. How are requirements conflicts resolved?

541. What method of measurement do you use?

542. Is there a set of procedures to capture, analyze and act on quality metrics?

543. Where is quality now?

544. If the defect rate during testing is substantially higher than that of the previous release (or a similar product), then ask: Did you plan for and actually improve testing effectiveness?

545. Do you know how much profit a 10% decrease in waste would generate?

546. Is material complete (and does it meet the standards)?

547. What are your organizations next steps?

548. What percentage are outcome-based?

549. Have alternatives been defined in the event that failure occurs?

550. Why is now the time for quality metrics?

2.26 Process Improvement Plan: Risk Ownership

551. What personnel are the sponsors for that initiative?

552. Are you following the quality standards?

553. What personnel are the change agents for your initiative?

554. Has a process guide to collect the data been developed?

555. Are you making progress on the improvement framework?

556. Who should prepare the process improvement action plan?

557. What makes people good SPI coaches?

558. Are you meeting the quality standards?

559. Where do you focus?

560. The motive is determined by asking, Why do you want to achieve this goal?

561. What lessons have you learned so far?

562. Have storage and access mechanisms and procedures been determined?

563. What is the return on investment?

564. Everyone agrees on what process improvement is, right?

565. Does your process ensure quality?

566. Why do you want to achieve the goal?

567. What actions are needed to address the problems and achieve the goals?

568. Where are you now?

569. Have the supporting tools been developed or acquired?

2.27 Responsibility Assignment Matrix: Risk Ownership

570. Too many as: does a proper segregation of duties exist?

571. The staff characteristics – is the group or the person capable to work together as a team?

572. Who is the sponsor?

573. What is the justification?

574. Do managers and team members provide helpful suggestions during review meetings?

575. Are there any drawbacks to using a responsibility assignment matrix?

576. How many people do you need?

577. Are too many reports done in writing instead of verbally?

578. Are records maintained to show how undistributed budgets are controlled?

579. What are some important Risk Ownership project communications management tools?

580. Are management actions taken to reduce indirect costs when there are significant adverse variances?

581. What do you do when people do not respond?

582. Availability – will the group or the person be available within the necessary time interval?

583. What is the business need?

584. Are people encouraged to bring up issues?

585. Does the contractor use objective results, design reviews, and tests to trace schedule?

586. What travel needed?

2.28 Roles and Responsibilities: Risk Ownership

587. Is the data complete?

588. What should you do now to prepare yourself for a promotion, increased responsibilities or a different job?

589. Are Risk Ownership project team roles and responsibilities identified and documented?

590. Do the values and practices inherent in the culture of your organization foster or hinder the process?

591. Was the expectation clearly communicated?

592. What areas of supervision are challenging for you?

593. Are your policies supportive of a culture of quality data?

594. What specific behaviors did you observe?

595. To decide whether to use a quality measurement, ask how will you know when it is achieved?

596. How is your work-life balance?

597. Accountabilities: what are the roles and responsibilities of individual team members?

598. Key conclusions and recommendations: Are conclusions and recommendations relevant and acceptable?

599. Be specific; avoid generalities. Thank you and great work alone are insufficient. What exactly do you appreciate and why?

600. Are your budgets supportive of a culture of quality data?

601. What is working well?

602. Once the responsibilities are defined for the Risk Ownership project, have the deliverables, roles and responsibilities been clearly communicated to every participant?

603. What expectations were met?

604. Does the team have access to and ability to use data analysis tools?

605. Concern: where are you limited or have no authority, where you can not influence?

606. What expectations were NOT met?

2.29 Human Resource Management Plan: Risk Ownership

607. Are non-critical path items updated and agreed upon with the teams?

608. Has the scope management document been updated and distributed to help prevent scope creep?

609. Is this Risk Ownership project carried out in partnership with other groups/organizations?

610. Who are the people that make up your organization and whom create the success that your organization enjoys as a whole?

611. Are adequate resources provided for the quality assurance function?

612. Were decisions made in a timely manner?

613. Are the right people being attracted and retained to meet the future challenges?

614. Are actuals compared against estimates to analyze and correct variances?

615. Does the detailed work plan match the complexity of tasks with the capabilities of personnel?

616. Is the structure for tracking the Risk Ownership project schedule well defined and assigned to a specific individual?

617. Are assumptions being identified, recorded, analyzed, qualified and closed?

618. How do you determine what key skills and talents are needed to meet the objectives. Is your organization primarily focused on a specific industry?

619. Based on your Risk Ownership project communication management plan, what worked well?

620. Do all stakeholders know how to access this repository and where to find the Risk Ownership project documentation?

621. Is the current culture aligned with the vision, mission, and values of the department?

622. What areas were overlooked on this Risk Ownership project?

623. Is it possible to track all classes of Risk Ownership project work (e.g. scheduled, un-scheduled, defect repair, etc.)?

624. Are procurement deliverables arriving on time and to specification?

2.30 Communications Management Plan: Risk Ownership

625. What is Risk Ownership project communications management?

626. Is there an important stakeholder who is actively opposed and will not receive messages?

627. Are others needed?

628. Who to share with?

629. Do you have members of your team responsible for certain stakeholders?

630. Do you ask; can you recommend others for you to talk with about this initiative?

631. How were corresponding initiatives successful?

632. What communications method?

633. Which stakeholders are thought leaders, influences, or early adopters?

634. Timing: when do the effects of the communication take place?

635. What steps can you take for a positive relationship?

636. Who will use or be affected by the result of a Risk

Ownership project?

637. Are the stakeholders getting the information others need, are others consulted, are concerns addressed?

638. What data is going to be required?

639. Do you feel a register helps?

640. Why is stakeholder engagement important?

641. Do you then often overlook a key stakeholder or stakeholder group?

642. Will messages be directly related to the release strategy or phases of the Risk Ownership project?

643. How did the term stakeholder originate?

644. Who were proponents/opponents?

2.31 Risk Management Plan: Risk Ownership

645. Monitoring -what factors can you track that will enable you to determine if the risk is becoming more or less likely?

646. What can go wrong?

647. Where are you confronted with risks during the business phases?

648. How is risk monitoring performed?

649. Does the software engineering team have the right mix of skills?

650. Degree of confidence in estimated size estimate?

651. Why do you need to manage Risk Ownership project Risk?

652. Management -what contingency plans do you have if the risk becomes a reality?

653. Have you worked with the customer in the past?

654. Have top software and customer managers formally committed to support the Risk Ownership project?

655. What are the chances the event will occur?

656. Has something like this been done before?

657. Is the customer willing to participate in reviews?

658. Can the Risk Ownership project proceed without assuming the risk?

659. What will drive change?

660. Number of users of the product?

661. For software; does the software interface with new or unproven hardware or unproven vendor products?

662. How can you fix it?

663. Financial risk -can your organization afford to undertake the Risk Ownership project?

2.32 Risk Register: Risk Ownership

664. People risk -are people with appropriate skills available to help complete the Risk Ownership project?

665. When would you develop a risk register?

666. Is further information required before making a decision?

667. Recovery actions - planned actions taken once a risk has occurred to allow you to move on. What should you do after?

668. Cost/benefit – how much will the proposed mitigations cost and how does this cost compare with the potential cost of the risk event/situation should it occur?

669. How well are risks controlled?

670. Financial risk -can your organization afford to undertake the Risk Ownership project?

671. Market risk -will the new service or product be useful to your organization or marketable to others?

672. When is it going to be done?

673. When will it happen?

674. Are there any gaps in the evidence?

675. Are your objectives at risk?

676. Manageability – have mitigations to the risk been identified?

677. What may happen or not go according to plan?

678. Budget and schedule: what are the estimated costs and schedules for performing risk-related activities?

679. What further options might be available for responding to the risk?

680. What should the audit role be in establishing a risk management process?

681. Who is accountable?

682. What has changed since the last period?

683. Amongst the action plans and recommendations that you have to introduce are there some that could stop or delay the overall program?

2.33 Probability and Impact Assessment: Risk Ownership

684. Who are the international/overseas Risk Ownership project partners (equipment supplier/supplier/consultant/contractor) for this Risk Ownership project?

685. Prioritized components/features?

686. Are there any Risk Ownership projects similar to this one in existence?

687. What should be the gestation period for the Risk Ownership project with specific technology?

688. Have you ascribed a level of confidence to every critical technical objective?

689. Do the requirements require the creation of new algorithms?

690. Are the risk data timely and relevant?

691. How is the risk management process used in practice?

692. What would be the effect of slippage?

693. Are some people working on multiple Risk Ownership projects?

694. Risk urgency assessment -which of your risks

could occur soon, or require a longer planning time?

695. To what extent is the chosen technology maturing?

696. Risks should be identified during which phase of Risk Ownership project management life cycle?

697. Is the delay in one subRisk Ownership project going to affect another?

698. What will be the impact or consequence if the risk occurs?

699. Are the software tools integrated with each other?

700. Will there be an increase in the political conservatism?

701. Do you use diagramming techniques to show cause and effect?

702. What will be the likely political situation during the life of the Risk Ownership project?

703. Is the present organizational structure for handling the Risk Ownership project sufficient?

2.34 Probability and Impact Matrix: Risk Ownership

704. My Risk Ownership project leader has suddenly left your organization, what do you do?

705. Do you have a consistent repeatable process that is actually used?

706. What are the likely future requirements?

707. What things are likely to change?

708. What is the level of commitment and professionalism?

709. Are people attending meetings and doing work?

710. What is the level of experience available with your organization?

711. How should you structure risks?

712. What things might go wrong?

713. What action do you usually take against risks?

714. What did not work so well?

715. Can it be enlarged by drawing people from other areas of your organization?

716. Who are the owners?

717. How carefully have the potential competitors been identified?

718. What are the methods to deal with risks?

719. How are you working with risks?

720. The customer requests a change to the Risk Ownership project that would increase the Risk Ownership project risk. Which should you do before ass the others?

721. What will be the likely political situation during the life of the Risk Ownership project?

2.35 Risk Data Sheet: Risk Ownership

722. Has the most cost-effective solution been chosen?

723. What will be the consequences if it happens?

724. What do you know?

725. What can happen?

726. How can it happen?

727. What are your core values?

728. Risk of what?

729. Who has a vested interest in how you perform as your organization (our stakeholders)?

730. Do effective diagnostic tests exist?

731. What were the Causes that contributed?

732. Has a sensitivity analysis been carried out?

733. What is the likelihood of it happening?

734. What is the chance that it will happen?

735. Whom do you serve (customers)?

736. Is the data sufficiently specified in terms of the type of failure being analyzed, and its frequency or

probability?

737. How do you handle product safely?

738. Potential for recurrence?

739. If it happens, what are the consequences?

740. How reliable is the data source?

2.36 Procurement Management Plan: Risk Ownership

741. Are Risk Ownership project contact logs kept up to date?

742. What is a Risk Ownership project Management Plan?

743. Were sponsors and decision makers available when needed outside regularly scheduled meetings?

744. Has a quality assurance plan been developed for the Risk Ownership project?

745. Has the schedule been baselined?

746. What types of contracts will be used?

747. Are updated Risk Ownership project time & resource estimates reasonable based on the current Risk Ownership project stage?

748. Is there a procurement management plan in place?

749. Is the schedule updated on a periodic basis?

750. Are quality inspections and review activities listed in the Risk Ownership project schedule(s)?

751. Are there checklists created to determine if all quality processes are followed?

752. Are all key components of a Quality Assurance Plan present?

753. Have lessons learned been conducted after each Risk Ownership project release?

754. Has the budget been baselined?

755. Alignment to strategic goals & objectives?

756. Are parking lot items captured?

757. Are the results of quality assurance reviews provided to affected groups & individuals?

758. How will you coordinate Procurement with aspects of the Risk Ownership project?

2.37 Source Selection Criteria: Risk Ownership

759. When is it appropriate to issue a Draft Request for Proposal (DRFP)?

760. Do you consider all weaknesses, significant weaknesses, and deficiencies?

761. How are oral presentations documented?

762. What are the most common types of rating systems?

763. What evidence should be provided regarding proposal evaluations?

764. What is the role of counsel in the procurement process?

765. Does an evaluation need to include the identification of strengths and weaknesses?

766. Is the contracting office likely to receive more purchase requests for this item or service during the coming year?

767. What documentation should be used to support the selection decision?

768. What should a DRFP include?

769. Has all proposal data been loaded?

770. What is price analysis and when should it be performed?

771. How will you evaluate offerors proposals?

772. What are the limitations on pre-competitive range communications?

773. How important is cost in the source selection decision relative to past performance and technical considerations?

774. How do you encourage efficiency and consistency?

775. What is cost analysis and when should it be performed?

776. What documentation is necessary regarding electronic communications?

777. What are the most critical evaluation criteria that prove to be tiebreakers in the evaluation of proposals?

778. Is there collaboration among your evaluators?

2.38 Stakeholder Management Plan: Risk Ownership

779. Have the key functions and capabilities been defined and assigned to each release or iteration?

780. Does the Risk Ownership project have a Quality Culture?

781. Has a quality assurance plan been developed for the Risk Ownership project?

782. What is positive about the current process?

783. Does the Risk Ownership project have a formal Risk Ownership project Charter?

784. Has a sponsor been identified?

785. Have adequate resources been provided by management to ensure Risk Ownership project success?

786. Who might be involved in developing a charter?

787. When would you develop a Risk Ownership project Execution Plan?

788. Which risks pose the highest threat?

789. Why would you develop a Risk Ownership project Business Plan?

790. Were the budget estimates reasonable?

791. Were Risk Ownership project team members involved in the development of activity & task decomposition?

792. Who is responsible for accepting the reports produced by the process?

793. Is the quality assurance team identified?

2.39 Change Management Plan: Risk Ownership

794. Will the readiness criteria be met prior to the training roll out?

795. What new behaviours are required?

796. When does it make sense to customize?

797. Impact of systems implementation on organization change?

798. Is there a software application relevant to this deliverable?

799. Where do you want to be?

800. Who in the business it includes?

801. Has the training co-ordinator been provided with the training details and put in place the necessary arrangements?

802. Have the business unit contacts been selected and notified?

803. Do the proposed users have access to the appropriate documentation?

804. Who will fund the training?

805. Is it the same for each of the business units?

806. Who might present the most resistance?

807. Has a training need analysis been carried out?

808. What will be the preferred method of delivery?

809. How will you deal with anger about the restricting of communications due to confidentiality considerations?

810. What would be an estimate of the total cost for the activities required to carry out the change initiative?

811. Who might be able to help you the most?

3.0 Executing Process Group: Risk Ownership

812. Does the case present a realistic scenario?

813. Who are the Risk Ownership project stakeholders?

814. How many different communication channels does the Risk Ownership project team have?

815. What are the main processes included in Risk Ownership project quality management?

816. Do Risk Ownership project managers understand your organizational context for Risk Ownership projects?

817. What type of people would you want on your team?

818. Does the Risk Ownership project team have enough people to execute the Risk Ownership project plan?

819. Just how important is your work to the overall success of the Risk Ownership project?

820. What are the Risk Ownership project management deliverables of each process group?

821. How can software assist in Risk Ownership project communications?

822. How does a Risk Ownership project life cycle differ from a product life cycle?

823. How do you control progress of your Risk Ownership project?

824. How does Risk Ownership project management relate to other disciplines?

825. What is the shortest possible time it will take to complete this Risk Ownership project?

826. What are the main types of contracts if you do decide to outsource?

827. What areas were overlooked on this Risk Ownership project?

828. Who will provide training?

829. What does it mean to take a systems view of a Risk Ownership project?

3.1 Team Member Status Report: Risk Ownership

830. Does the product, good, or service already exist within your organization?

831. When a teams productivity and success depend on collaboration and the efficient flow of information, what generally fails them?

832. How does this product, good, or service meet the needs of the Risk Ownership project and your organization as a whole?

833. Will the staff do training or is that done by a third party?

834. Is there evidence that staff is taking a more professional approach toward management of your organizations Risk Ownership projects?

835. Do you have an Enterprise Risk Ownership project Management Office (EPMO)?

836. What is to be done?

837. The problem with Reward & Recognition Programs is that the truly deserving people all too often get left out. How can you make it practical?

838. Why is it to be done?

839. Does every department have to have a Risk

Ownership project Manager on staff?

840. Are the products of your organizations Risk Ownership projects meeting customers objectives?

841. How much risk is involved?

842. How it is to be done?

843. How will resource planning be done?

844. Does your organization have the means (staff, money, contract, etc.) to produce or to acquire the product, good, or service?

845. Are the attitudes of staff regarding Risk Ownership project work improving?

846. What specific interest groups do you have in place?

847. Are your organizations Risk Ownership projects more successful over time?

848. How can you make it practical?

3.2 Change Request: Risk Ownership

849. What can be filed?

850. Does the schedule include Risk Ownership project management time and change request analysis time?

851. How are changes graded and who is responsible for the rating?

852. How is the change documented (format, content, storage)?

853. Why were your requested changes rejected or not made?

854. Will all change requests and current status be logged?

855. Are there requirements attributes that can discriminate between high and low reliability?

856. Will all change requests be unconditionally tracked through this process?

857. Who is responsible to authorize changes?

858. Has the change been highlighted and documented in the CSCI?

859. Will there be a change request form in use?

860. What is the purpose of change control?

861. How to get changes (code) out in a timely manner?

862. Who is included in the change control team?

863. What are the requirements for urgent changes?

864. What is a Change Request Form?

865. When do you create a change request?

866. What is the relationship between requirements attributes and attributes like complexity and size?

867. How are changes requested (forms, method of communication)?

868. Has your address changed?

3.3 Change Log: Risk Ownership

869. Is the requested change request a result of changes in other Risk Ownership project(s)?

870. Should a more thorough impact analysis be conducted?

871. Does the suggested change request seem to represent a necessary enhancement to the product?

872. Is the submitted change a new change or a modification of a previously approved change?

873. How does this relate to the standards developed for specific business processes?

874. Is the change request open, closed or pending?

875. How does this change affect scope?

876. Who initiated the change request?

877. When was the request approved?

878. Do the described changes impact on the integrity or security of the system?

879. Is this a mandatory replacement?

880. How does this change affect the timeline of the schedule?

881. Will the Risk Ownership project fail if the change

request is not executed?

882. When was the request submitted?

883. Is the change request within Risk Ownership project scope?

884. Is the change backward compatible without limitations?

3.4 Decision Log: Risk Ownership

885. Do strategies and tactics aimed at less than full control reduce the costs of management or simply shift the cost burden?

886. What alternatives/risks were considered?

887. How does an increasing emphasis on cost containment influence the strategies and tactics used?

888. Does anything need to be adjusted?

889. How consolidated and comprehensive a story can you tell by capturing currently available incident data in a central location and through a log of key decisions during an incident?

890. Who will be given a copy of this document and where will it be kept?

891. How does the use a Decision Support System influence the strategies/tactics or costs?

892. With whom was the decision shared or considered?

893. What are the cost implications?

894. Is everything working as expected?

895. What is the average size of your matters in an applicable measurement?

896. What is your overall strategy for quality control / quality assurance procedures?

897. At what point in time does loss become unacceptable?

898. How do you define success?

899. Decision-making process; how will the team make decisions?

900. What makes you different or better than others companies selling the same thing?

901. Behaviors; what are guidelines that the team has identified that will assist them with getting the most out of team meetings?

902. What eDiscovery problem or issue did your organization set out to fix or make better?

903. What was the rationale for the decision?

904. How does provision of information, both in terms of content and presentation, influence acceptance of alternative strategies?

3.5 Quality Audit: Risk Ownership

905. Are all staff empowered and encouraged to contribute to ongoing improvement efforts?

906. How does your organization know that its staff embody the core knowledge, skills and characteristics for which it wishes to be recognized?

907. How does your organization know that its public relations and marketing systems are appropriately effective and constructive?

908. How does your organization know that its advisory services are appropriately effective and constructive?

909. How does the organization know that its industry and community engagement planning and management systems are appropriately effective and constructive in enabling relationships with key stakeholder groups?

910. How does your organization know that it is appropriately effective and constructive in preparing its staff for organizational aspirations?

911. Does everyone know what they are supposed to be doing, how and why?

912. How does your organization know that its financial management system is appropriately effective and constructive?

913. How does your organization know that its policy management system is appropriately effective and constructive?

914. How are you auditing your organizations compliance with regulations?

915. Is your organizations resource allocation system properly aligned with its collection of intentions?

916. Is the reports overall tone appropriate?

917. How does your organization know that its planning processes are appropriately effective and constructive?

918. How does your organization know that its security arrangements are appropriately effective and constructive?

919. How does your organization know that its staff placements are appropriately effective and constructive in relation to program-related learning outcomes?

920. How does your organization know that its promotions system is appropriately effective, constructive and fair?

921. What are you trying to do?

922. What review processes are in place for your organizations major activities?

923. Why are you trying to do it?

924. What does the organizarion look for in a Quality audit?

3.6 Team Directory: Risk Ownership

925. Where will the product be used and/or delivered or built when appropriate?

926. Process decisions: is work progressing on schedule and per contract requirements?

927. How and in what format should information be presented?

928. Who are your stakeholders (customers, sponsors, end users, team members)?

929. How will you accomplish and manage the objectives?

930. What are you going to deliver or accomplish?

931. Who will write the meeting minutes and distribute?

932. Timing: when do the effects of communication take place?

933. When will you produce deliverables?

934. Who will talk to the customer?

935. What needs to be communicated?

936. Process decisions: do invoice amounts match accepted work in place?

937. Is construction on schedule?

938. Process decisions: do job conditions warrant additional actions to collect job information and document on-site activity?

939. Decisions: is the most suitable form of contract being used?

940. Where should the information be distributed?

941. When does information need to be distributed?

942. Process decisions: which organizational elements and which individuals will be assigned management functions?

943. Decisions: what could be done better to improve the quality of the constructed product?

3.7 Team Operating Agreement: Risk Ownership

944. Are there more than two national cultures represented by your team?

945. Do you determine the meeting length and time of day?

946. What is group supervision?

947. Do you use a parking lot for any items that are important and outside of the agenda?

948. What individual strengths does each team member bring to the group?

949. Do you call or email participants to ensure understanding, follow-through and commitment to the meeting outcomes?

950. Do you post meeting notes and the recording (if used) and notify participants?

951. Is compensation based on team and individual performance?

952. Does your team need access to all documents and information at all times?

953. Are there more than two native languages represented by your team?

954. Do you leverage technology engagement tools group chat, polls, screen sharing, etc.?

955. Do team members reside in more than two countries?

956. Seconds for members to respond?

957. Are leadership responsibilities shared among team members (versus a single leader)?

958. Have you set the goals and objectives of the team?

959. Do you ask participants to close laptops and place mobile devices on silent on the table while the meeting is in progress?

960. Did you delegate tasks such as taking meeting minutes, presenting a topic and soliciting input?

961. Do you listen for voice tone and word choice to understand the meaning behind words?

962. What is the anticipated procedure (recruitment, solicitation of volunteers, or assignment) for selecting team members?

963. How will you resolve conflict efficiently and respectfully?

3.8 Team Performance Assessment: Risk Ownership

964. To what degree does the teams work approach provide opportunity for members to engage in open interaction?

965. How hard did you try to make a good selection?

966. To what degree do members articulate the goals beyond the team membership?

967. To what degree do team members agree with the goals, relative importance, and the ways in which achievement will be measured?

968. How hard do you try to make a good selection?

969. To what degree do team members articulate the teams work approach?

970. How much interpersonal friction is there in your team?

971. To what degree will new and supplemental skills be introduced as the need is recognized?

972. To what degree do the goals specify concrete team work products?

973. To what degree are the skill areas critical to team performance present?

974. To what degree will the team ensure that all members equitably share the work essential to the success of the team?

975. What are teams?

976. To what degree are the goals ambitious?

977. To what degree does the team possess adequate membership to achieve its ends?

978. To what degree can team members vigorously define the teams purpose in considerations with others who are not part of the functioning team?

979. What do you think is the most constructive thing that could be done now to resolve considerations and disputes about method variance?

980. Can team performance be reliably measured in simulator and live exercises using the same assessment tool?

981. Individual task proficiency and team process behavior: what is important for team functioning?

982. What is method variance?

983. Does more radicalness mean more perceived benefits?

3.9 Team Member Performance Assessment: Risk Ownership

984. How do you use data to inform instruction and improve staff achievement?

985. What were the challenges that resulted for training and assessment?

986. What instructional strategies were developed/ incorporated (e.g., direct instruction, indirect instruction, experiential learning, independent study, interactive instruction)?

987. How does your team work together?

988. Can your organization rate by exception and assume that most employees are performing at an acceptable level?

989. Are any governance changes sufficient to impact achievement?

990. How do you currently account for your results in the teams achievement?

991. How effective is training that is delivered through technology-based platforms?

992. How are training activities developed from a technical perspective?

993. What is the role of the Reviewer?

994. What specific plans do you have for developing effective cross-platform assessments in a blended learning environment?

995. What is the Business Management Oversight Process?

996. What makes them effective?

997. How is performance assessment used in making future award decisions including options and extend/compete decisions?

998. What resources do you need?

999. What variables that affect team members achievement are within your control?

1000. Verify business objectives. Are they appropriate, and well-articulated?

1001. To what degree are the goals realistic?

1002. To what degree can the team measure progress against specific goals?

3.10 Issue Log: Risk Ownership

1003. Where do team members get information?

1004. Are the stakeholders getting the information they need, are they consulted, are concerns addressed?

1005. Who reported the issue?

1006. Do you feel more overwhelmed by stakeholders?

1007. How often do you engage with stakeholders?

1008. Do you prepare stakeholder engagement plans?

1009. What is a Stakeholder?

1010. Why multiple evaluators?

1011. Who is the stakeholder?

1012. Persistence; will users learn a work around or will they be bothered every time?

1013. In classifying stakeholders, which approach to do so are you using?

1014. Who have you worked with in past, similar initiatives?

1015. Are you constantly rushing from meeting to meeting?

1016. Is access to the Issue Log controlled?

1017. What effort will a change need?

1018. Are the Risk Ownership project issues uniquely identified, including to which product they refer?

1019. What is the status of the issue?

1020. Do you often overlook a key stakeholder or stakeholder group?

1021. Why do you manage communications?

1022. What is the impact on the risks?

4.0 Monitoring and Controlling Process Group: Risk Ownership

1023. Is progress on outcomes due to your program?

1024. Do the partners have sufficient financial capacity to keep up the benefits produced by the programme?

1025. What resources (both financial and non-financial) are available/needed?

1026. Change, where should you look for problems?

1027. How is Agile Risk Ownership project Management done?

1028. What kinds of things in particular are you looking for data on?

1029. Is there sufficient time allotted between the general system design and the detailed system design phases?

1030. Where is the Risk in the Risk Ownership project?

1031. How do you monitor progress?

1032. What are the goals of the program?

1033. How is agile program management done?

1034. Who needs to be involved in the planning?

1035. If a risk event occurs, what will you do?

1036. How can you monitor progress?

1037. When will the Risk Ownership project be done?

1038. What were things that you did very well and want to do the same again on the next Risk Ownership project?

1039. Specific - is the objective clear in terms of what, how, when, and where the situation will be changed?

1040. Based on your Risk Ownership project communication management plan, what worked well?

4.1 Project Performance Report: Risk Ownership

1041. To what degree can the team ensure that all members are individually and jointly accountable for the teams purpose, goals, approach, and work-products?

1042. To what degree will team members, individually and collectively, commit time to help themselves and others learn and develop skills?

1043. How can Risk Ownership project sustainability be maintained?

1044. To what degree do team members feel that the purpose of the team is important, if not exciting?

1045. To what degree does the teams purpose contain themes that are particularly meaningful and memorable?

1046. To what degree do team members frequently explore the teams purpose and its implications?

1047. What is the PRS?

1048. To what degree are the demands of the task compatible with and converge with the mission and functions of the formal organization?

1049. To what degree are the tasks requirements reflected in the flow and storage of information?

1050. To what degree can team members meet frequently enough to accomplish the teams ends?

1051. To what degree can team members frequently and easily communicate with one another?

1052. To what degree are the structures of the formal organization consistent with the behaviors in the informal organization?

1053. To what degree can the cognitive capacity of individuals accommodate the flow of information?

1054. To what degree does the task meet individual needs?

1055. To what degree will each member have the opportunity to advance his or her professional skills in all three of the above categories while contributing to the accomplishment of the teams purpose and goals?

1056. To what degree is there centralized control of information sharing?

1057. Next Steps?

4.2 Variance Analysis: Risk Ownership

1058. Are data elements reconcilable between internal summary reports and reports forwarded to the stakeholders?

1059. What does a favorable labor efficiency variance mean?

1060. Is cost and schedule performance measurement done in a consistent, systematic manner?

1061. Are the wbs and organizational levels for application of the Risk Ownership projected overhead costs identified?

1062. What should management do?

1063. What is the actual cost of work performed?

1064. Are all authorized tasks assigned to identified organizational elements?

1065. What business event causes fluctuations?

1066. Budget versus actual. how does the monthly budget compare to actual experience?

1067. Are there externalities from having some customers, even if they are unprofitable in the short run?

1068. Does the accounting system provide a basis for auditing records of direct costs chargeable to the contract?

1069. Who are responsible for overhead performance control of related costs?

1070. At what point should variances be isolated and brought to the attention of the management?

1071. Historical experience?

1072. There are detailed schedules which support control account and work package start and completion dates/events?

1073. What is the incurrence of actual indirect costs in excess of budgets, by element of expense?

1074. Are there knowledgeable Risk Ownership projections of future performance?

1075. Are procedures for variance analysis documented and consistently applied at the control account level and selected WBS and organizational levels at least monthly as a routine task?

4.3 Earned Value Status: Risk Ownership

1076. What is the unit of forecast value?

1077. Where are your problem areas?

1078. How much is it going to cost by the finish?

1079. Where is evidence-based earned value in your organization reported?

1080. Validation is a process of ensuring that the developed system will actually achieve the stakeholders desired outcomes; Are you building the right product? What do you validate?

1081. When is it going to finish?

1082. Verification is a process of ensuring that the developed system satisfies the stakeholders agreements and specifications; Are you building the product right? What do you verify?

1083. If earned value management (EVM) is so good in determining the true status of a Risk Ownership project and Risk Ownership project its completion, why is it that hardly any one uses it in information systems related Risk Ownership projects?

1084. Earned value can be used in almost any Risk Ownership project situation and in almost any Risk Ownership project environment. it may be used on large Risk Ownership projects, medium sized Risk Ownership projects, tiny Risk Ownership projects (in cut-down form), complex and simple Risk Ownership projects and in any market sector. some people, of course, know all about earned value, they have used it for years - but perhaps not as effectively as they could have?

1085. Are you hitting your Risk Ownership projects targets?

1086. How does this compare with other Risk Ownership projects?

4.4 Risk Audit: Risk Ownership

1087. Do you have a clear plan for the future that describes what you want to do and how you are going to do it?

1088. Are you willing to seek legal advice when required?

1089. Which assets are important?

1090. Do industry specialists and business risk auditors enhance audit reporting accuracy?

1091. Should additional substantive testing be conducted because of the risk audit results?

1092. Are audit program plans risk-adjusted?

1093. Are tool mentors available?

1094. Are all financial transactions accurately recorded (receipted, banked)?

1095. Assessing risk with analytical procedures: do systemsthinking tools help auditors focus on diagnostic patterns?

1096. Does the adoption of a business risk audit approach change internal control documentation and testing practices?

1097. Strategic business risk audit methodologies; are corresponding an attempt to sell other services, and is management becoming the client of the audit rather than the shareholder?

1098. Have risks been considered with an insurance broker or provider and suitable insurance cover been arranged?

1099. Are procedures developed to respond to foreseeable emergencies and communicated to all involved?

1100. Are procedures in place to ensure the security of staff and information and compliance with privacy legislation if applicable?

1101. Do you conduct risk assessments on all programs, activities and events?

1102. Does your board meet regularly and document all decisions and actions?

1103. Are formal technical reviews part of this process?

1104. Does the team have the right mix of skills?

1105. How are risk appetites expressed?

1106. Is your organization willing to commit significant time to the requirements gathering process?

4.5 Contractor Status Report: Risk Ownership

1107. If applicable; describe your standard schedule for new software version releases. Are new software version releases included in the standard maintenance plan?

1108. Describe how often regular updates are made to the proposed solution. Are corresponding regular updates included in the standard maintenance plan?

1109. How does the proposed individual meet each requirement?

1110. What was the overall budget or estimated cost?

1111. What are the minimum and optimal bandwidth requirements for the proposed solution?

1112. What process manages the contracts?

1113. What was the budget or estimated cost for your organizations services?

1114. How long have you been using the services?

1115. How is risk transferred?

1116. What is the average response time for answering a support call?

1117. Are there contractual transfer concerns?

1118. What was the final actual cost?

1119. Who can list a Risk Ownership project as organization experience, your organization or a previous employee of your organization?

1120. What was the actual budget or estimated cost for your organizations services?

4.6 Formal Acceptance: Risk Ownership

1121. Was the Risk Ownership project managed well?

1122. What was done right?

1123. What is the Acceptance Management Process?

1124. Do you buy-in installation services?

1125. Do you buy pre-configured systems or build your own configuration?

1126. How does your team plan to obtain formal acceptance on your Risk Ownership project?

1127. Was the Risk Ownership project goal achieved?

1128. What can you do better next time?

1129. Do you perform formal acceptance or burn-in tests?

1130. Was the client satisfied with the Risk Ownership project results?

1131. Is formal acceptance of the Risk Ownership project product documented and distributed?

1132. Was the sponsor/customer satisfied?

1133. General estimate of the costs and times to

complete the Risk Ownership project?

1134. How well did the team follow the methodology?

1135. What lessons were learned about your Risk Ownership project management methodology?

1136. Does it do what Risk Ownership project team said it would?

1137. Did the Risk Ownership project manager and team act in a professional and ethical manner?

1138. Does it do what client said it would?

1139. Have all comments been addressed?

1140. Who supplies data?

5.0 Closing Process Group: Risk Ownership

1141. Did the Risk Ownership project team have enough people to execute the Risk Ownership project plan?

1142. Measurable - are the targets measurable?

1143. How critical is the Risk Ownership project success to the success of your organization?

1144. How will staff learn how to use the deliverables?

1145. What is an Encumbrance?

1146. What is the overall risk of the Risk Ownership project to your organization?

1147. What could have been improved?

1148. What level of risk does the proposed budget represent to the Risk Ownership project?

1149. How well defined and documented were the Risk Ownership project management processes you chose to use?

1150. Did you do things well?

1151. What is the risk of failure to your organization?

1152. Was the schedule met?

1153. How well did you do?

1154. Did the delivered product meet the specified requirements and goals of the Risk Ownership project?

1155. How well did the team follow the chosen processes?

1156. Based on your Risk Ownership project communication management plan, what worked well?

5.1 Procurement Audit: Risk Ownership

1157. Has it been determined how large a portion of the procurement portfolio should be managed by the procurement function/unit and how large a portion that should be managed locally?

1158. Are idle funds invested, and is interest distributed to the various activity accounts at least annually?

1159. Are regulations and protective measures in place to avoid corruption?

1160. Are regulations on taxes, fees, duties, excises, tariffs etc. not impeding (international) competition?

1161. Is the opportunity properly published?

1162. Does procurement staff have recognized professional procurement qualifications or sufficient training?

1163. Were any additional works or deliveries admissible without the need for a new procurement procedure?

1164. Is there no evidence of collusion between bidders?

1165. Is there no evidence of favouritism towards a particular contractor during the evaluation and negotiation processes?

1166. Does the department evaluate and benchmark the performance of the procurement function/ unit against other comparable procurement functions/ units?

1167. Is the purchasing department facility laid out to facilitate interviews with salespersons?

1168. Are internal control systems in place?

1169. Is a cost/benefit analysis, a cost/effectiveness or a financial analysis considering life-cycle costs performed and is the funding of the procurement guaranteed?

1170. Were no tenders presented after the time limit accepted?

1171. Access to data, including standing data, and the identification of restriction levels and authorised personnel was in place?

1172. Does the procurement Risk Ownership project comply with European Communities regulations and rules?

1173. Is data securely stored?

1174. Are all claims certified by the officer giving rise to the claim (usually the purchasing agent)?

1175. Are unusual uses of organization funds investigated?

1176. Were exclusion causes duly considered before the actual evaluation of tenders?

5.2 Contract Close-Out: Risk Ownership

1177. Have all contracts been closed?

1178. What happens to the recipient of services?

1179. Are the signers the authorized officials?

1180. How does it work?

1181. Was the contract type appropriate?

1182. Change in knowledge?

1183. Was the contract sufficiently clear so as not to result in numerous disputes and misunderstandings?

1184. Parties: who is involved?

1185. Have all contract records been included in the Risk Ownership project archives?

1186. Have all contracts been completed?

1187. How/when used ?

1188. Parties: Authorized?

1189. Change in circumstances?

1190. Was the contract complete without requiring numerous changes and revisions?

1191. Change in attitude or behavior?

1192. What is capture management?

1193. Has each contract been audited to verify acceptance and delivery?

1194. Have all acceptance criteria been met prior to final payment to contractors?

1195. How is the contracting office notified of the automatic contract close-out?

5.3 Project or Phase Close-Out: Risk Ownership

1196. What are they?

1197. In preparing the Lessons Learned report, should it reflect a consensus viewpoint, or should the report reflect the different individual viewpoints?

1198. What can you do better next time, and what specific actions can you take to improve?

1199. Who controlled the resources for the Risk Ownership project?

1200. Who is responsible for award close-out?

1201. Were messages directly related to the release strategy or phases of the Risk Ownership project?

1202. In addition to assessing whether the Risk Ownership project was successful, it is equally critical to analyze why it was or was not fully successful. Are you including this?

1203. Is the lesson based on actual Risk Ownership project experience rather than on independent research?

1204. What were the desired outcomes?

1205. Who are the Risk Ownership project stakeholders and what are roles and involvement?

1206. What was expected from each stakeholder?

1207. Which changes might a stakeholder be required to make as a result of the Risk Ownership project?

1208. Did the Risk Ownership project management methodology work?

1209. Who exerted influence that has positively affected or negatively impacted the Risk Ownership project?

1210. What could be done to improve the process?

1211. Is the lesson significant, valid, and applicable?

1212. Planned completion date?

1213. What benefits or impacts does the stakeholder group expect to obtain as a result of the Risk Ownership project?

1214. What information is each stakeholder group interested in?

5.4 Lessons Learned: Risk Ownership

1215. What report generation capability is needed?

1216. What were the main sources of frustration in the Risk Ownership project?

1217. How well do you feel the executives supported this Risk Ownership project?

1218. What are the conceptual limits of the research?

1219. Where do you go from here?

1220. Was the control overhead justified?

1221. How much communication is socially oriented?

1222. What data are likely to be missing?

1223. What are the internal fiscal constraints?

1224. What were the problems encountered in the Risk Ownership project-functional area relationship, why, and how could they be fixed?

1225. For the next Risk Ownership project, how could you improve on the way Risk Ownership project was conducted?

1226. How effectively were issues managed on the Risk Ownership project?

1227. Was sufficient time allocated to review Risk

Ownership project deliverables?

1228. What is the supervisor to staff ratio?

1229. Whom to share Lessons Learned Information with?

1230. What would you approach differently next time?

1231. How useful and complete was the Risk Ownership project document repository?

1232. How much time is required for the task?

1233. How effective were Risk Ownership project audits?

Index

impact 4, 38, 45-46, 51, 54, 56, 85, 133, 168, 180-181, 200-202, 212, 220, 233, 236
impacted   146, 148, 259
impacts   45, 133, 148, 259
impeding   253
implement   19, 55, 69, 90, 139
implicit 107
importance   231
important   19, 24, 31, 64, 68-69, 103, 109, 115, 118, 130, 133, 167, 180, 184, 188, 194-195, 209, 214, 229, 232, 239, 245
improve   2, 9, 72, 74-77, 80-81, 83, 85-87, 89, 125, 166, 182, 185, 228, 233, 258-260
improved   78-79, 81, 86, 90, 251
improving   84, 217
incentives   93
incident   222
include   18, 84, 139, 208, 218
included   2, 7, 20, 44, 178, 214, 219, 247, 256
includes   9, 138, 212
including   25, 32, 40-41, 54, 61, 77, 98, 100, 147, 234, 236, 254, 258
increase   77, 121, 201, 203
increased   109, 190
increasing   115, 222
incurrence   242
incurring   152
in-depth   8, 10
indicate   67, 95, 114
indicated   94
indicators   24, 55, 64, 66, 69, 72, 86, 99
indirect   46, 152, 188, 233, 242
indirectly   1
individual   1, 170, 190, 192, 229, 232, 240, 247, 258
industry   99, 108, 115, 154, 161, 193, 224, 245
infinite 108
influence   86, 117, 129, 191, 222-223, 259
influences   194
inform 233
informal   240
informed   118, 125
ingrained   94
inherent   190
initial   32, 119, 183

problems   16, 19-20, 24-25, 78, 82, 84, 94, 133, 141-142, 187,
237, 260
procedure   230, 253
procedures   9, 86, 94-95, 100, 138, 152, 155, 164, 182-184, 186,
223, 242, 245-246
proceed   197
process   1-7, 9, 28-31, 37, 59-69, 71-72, 79-80, 90-91, 93-97,
99-100, 125, 132, 138-139, 141-143, 146, 148, 154-155, 164, 168-
170, 175, 180, 182-183, 186-187, 190, 199-200, 202, 208, 210-211,
214, 218, 223, 227-228, 232, 234, 237, 243, 246-247, 249, 251, 259
processes   46, 59, 61-62, 64, 66-67, 69-72, 93, 95, 100, 132-
133, 147-148, 206, 214, 220, 225, 251-252, 254
produce   69, 133, 164, 177, 217, 227
produced   59, 80, 211, 237
producing   143, 146
product   1, 51, 64, 69, 109, 119, 132-133, 139, 146-147, 161,
172, 185, 197-198, 205, 215-217, 220, 227-228, 236, 243, 249, 252
production   37, 80, 109
products   1, 18, 22, 54, 106, 120, 132, 143, 181, 197, 217,
231
profit   185
program   22, 46, 70, 99, 132, 135, 199, 237, 245
programme   237
programs   133, 216, 246
progress   31, 54, 84, 98, 103, 123, 132, 146, 175, 179, 186,
215, 230, 234, 237-238
project 2-8, 19, 21-22, 25, 35, 53, 64, 70, 73, 78, 96, 98, 100, 103,
107, 109, 112, 114, 116, 124-133, 135-138, 140, 142-143, 145-150,
154-163, 166-176, 178-182, 188, 190-198, 200-203, 206-207, 210-
211, 214-218, 220-221, 236-239, 243, 248-252, 254, 256, 258-261
projected   151, 241
projects   2, 48, 117, 119, 124, 127, 131, 133, 143, 145, 149,
169, 173, 182, 200, 214, 216-217, 243-244
promising   109
promote   54, 58, 130
promotion   190
promotions   225
proofing   80
proper 90, 188
properly   41, 125, 152, 225, 253
proponents   195
proposal   140, 160-161, 208
proposals   95, 169, 209

CPSIA information can be obtained
at www.ICGtesting.com
Printed in the USA
BVHW040428130819
555624BV00049B/1879/P

9 780655 839767